"The CEO Code *is the book every executive,* and *executive assistant needs to have on their bedstand or in their desk drawer. David Rohlander—fighter pilot, seasoned executive, successful entrepreneur, management coach, and practical philosopher—writes with rare insight and empathy, drawing together gripping personal examples, real-world case studies, lessons learned over a lifetime of executive experiences and practical tips that anyone aspiring to a leadership position should know.*

Senior readers will finish this outstanding book wishing they had it when they began their careers. Those starting out will find that it will become a constant and reliable companion, their appreciation for its wisdom and its remarkable author increasing over the years."

—Dr. Richard P. Hallion, aerospace historian, consultant, and retired Air Force senior executive

"Rohlander has certainly cracked the code for CEOs in his newest book. As any CEO, or aspiring CEO, reads The CEO Code, *light bulbs will illuminate on how to master communication, execution, and operations in order to build a better company. I especially like the end-of-chapter Take Time to Reflect questions that help internalize and personalize what you've just read. This book should be a part of every CEO's library!"*

—Dr. Tony Alessandra, hall-of-fame keynote speaker and author of *The New Art of Managing People and Communicating at Work*

"Organizations that have CEOs and leaders with vision, compassion and great communication skills always have an edge on their competition. As a former CEO I know how my behavior and open communication influenced what employees and stakeholders understood and believed. David Rohlander has experienced the value of communication in his multifaceted career and lays out a flight plan that breaks it down into manageable pieces for success."

—Howard Putnam, former Southwest Airlines CEO, speaker and author of *The Winds of Turbulence*

"The CEO Code is an electrifying tour through the highways and byways of what it takes to be a great leader. More than a guidebook, it is a personal statement that will resonate with readers from all skill levels. Even the president of the United States could learn from this book. I know I did."

—William Cane, best-selling author of *Clubhouse Confidential*

"Even if you are a seasoned businessman or in the early stages of your career *The CEO Code provides a clear and concise blueprint to strengthen your organization's ability, to work better as a team and have fun at the same time! The methods you learn will result in developing and nurturing mutual trust and respect with others that will benefit you in both your professional and personal life.*"

—Roy Stephenson, PE, HR Green, manager—
local governmental services

"*The CEO Code is a great book with a great purpose to help you create a masterpiece in your personal and professional life. David, a former fighter pilot, has created a flight manual and a practical flight plan for you to activate on a daily basis. The emphasis on the critical skills of communication, execution, and operations takes the mystery out of high performance. The real-life examples he shares from his life experiences made me smile, think, and commit to engaging in the change process.*"

—Dan McBride, VP Wealth Teams Solutions,
former president of Jim Rohn Productions

"*Rohlander's writing is creative, his illustrative stories are delightful, and his valuable advice provides a proven roadmap. You can look better to both the people above you and below you at work. Read this book before returning to the office.*"

—Dan Poynter, author, publisher, and speaker

"*The CEO Code is right on the mark. It is an effective and practical guide to improving your performance that will help you reflect and think about changes you should make. Fun to read, you will learn new ways to achieve better results.*"

—Donald Natenstedt, regional managing partner, west region,
McGladrey LLP

"*David Rohlander has captured the scope of what makes a CEO a great leader and an inspiration to those he serves. It is not for the faint of heart. It is down to earth and practical and is especially useful to those who visualize themselves as worthy of the title.*"

—George Morrisey, CSP, CPAE Speaker Hall of Fame, author of
Creating Your Future and *Morrisey on Planning* three-book series

"*Been there—done that! If there's anyone who epitomizes those words, it is clearly David Rohlander! Coupled with a rich background in serving as CEO in the corporate sector, his varied and equally enriching role as a consultant to numerous other CEOs makes him the perfect author for this important book.*

And don't let the title fool you. It matters not if you're the CEO of a multinational organization or the CEO of your own life, the lessons you will learn are equally applicable. This highly readable work, while heavily research-based, is loaded with real-world scenarios and is an extremely practical guide to anyone interested in enhancing their interpersonal skills."

—Edward E. Scannell, CMP, CSP, coauthor, *Games Trainers Play* series,
Past National President; ASTD, IFTDO, MPI and NSA

"An old colleague of mine used to say people don't need to be taught; they need to be reminded. David Rohlander has some terrific reminders in this book of what it takes to be an effective CEO. Blending his background as a US Air Force pilot with decades of practical business experience, David offers up solid, sensible, do-able ideas that any of us who lead others can benefit from reviewing."

—Lou Heckler, business keynote speaker and speaker coach

"CEOs succeed when they are able to recognize patterns. Everything is coded. Rohlander pulls out the essentials for any CEO. Congratulations on grasping the CEO Code, pulling it out, seeing the analogical construct to basic codes as genetics, honor and the deepest values of life. All CEOs need a deep-seated code to guide them and here you have opened the door. Continuity, symmetry, and harmony only occur when those codes begin to work."

—Bruce Camber, CEO, Small Business School, over 50 seasons of
television on PBS-TV and VOA-TV

"David Rohlander's warm and caring personality comes through on every page of The CEO Code. *I especially like the common sense and simple way that he approaches the ever-important challenge of building teams. This book is easy to pick up. Not so easy to lay down. You'll enjoy it, but more importantly, you'll get very usable information from it."*

—Stephen W. Frueh, PhD, author of *From Marginal to Magnificent*

"I have known David Rohlander for many years. Habits make or break people. In this book you will learn how to master them. The CEO Code is based on David's own real experience. It is both pragmatic and useful. I teach senior executives of corporations that it is vital to differentiate between what people say and what they do. If you want your company to take a massive leap forward then The Ceo Code is a must-read."

—Charles Donoghue, FNZIM, APS, New Zealand's #1 performance
psychology coach, international speaker, author, and corporate trainer
www.charlesdonoghue.com

"David Rohlander is well-qualified to write about how to become an authentic and credible communicator. He has been there and done that. I met Dave 30 years ago and have been impressed with his ability to get to the heart of any matter and help other people do the same. Read this book and get ready for significant improvement in your communication ability and results—IMMEDIATELY!"

—Rex C. Houze, CEO, Improving Performance & Results, Inc., author of *Developing Personal Leadership*

"The information, analogies, and illustrations that David delivers in The CEO Code *are like a knowledge bomb! His insight on communication, how we are all communicating all the time, was eye opening. David provides you with the tools you need to be successful. No matter the field of business you're in, there's something in this book for you.*"

—Brian P. Murphy, CMCA, AMS, PCAM, president, Total Property Management, Inc.

"A great read. Finally a book that is practical, useful and shows you why, how and what to do to be a great leader. The CEO Code *is super helpful because it's based on real experience, achievements and failures. Fun to read!*"

—Rick Frishman, publisher, Morgan James Publishing, *www.rickfrishman.com*

"David Rohlander has written THE handbook for senior executive success. If you are a CEO, want to become a CEO, or simply want to master the habits of highly effective corporate and entrepreneurial leaders, this book is for you. David's advice in this book—just like his advice to his CEO coaching clients—is highly focused, concise, and powerful.

He doesn't waste a word on fluff or theory. This book is all meat and all highly relevant to today's business environment of uncertainty, dramatic change, and turbulence. The good news, David is both a U.S. Air Force veteran and veteran CEO so he's no stranger to turbulence of any kind!

Throughout the course of the book, David peppers his hard-hitting CEO-level advice with deep insights, great stories, and unexpected humor. If you are ready to take your business to new heights of financial, personal and professional success, The CEO Code *is a must-read.*"

—David Newman, author of *Do It! Marketing*

"Communication is essential for interacting with others yet very few of us are naturally born communicators. DGR delves into what makes a good communicator *and brings it across to his audience so that they can easily understand and improve their own communication skills."*

—Andrew Hafemeister, head of product delivery management misys, Paris, France

"Any serious student involved in leadership of others and of business has experienced a plethora of approaches in books: some pedantic as step-by-step approaches, often missing the interactive dynamics of human emotions; others overarching into misty ideals of spirituality, yet obtuse to implement into effective results.

In reading David G. Rohlander's The CEO Code, *I am excited to report that the author has managed to overcome the trap of setting boundaries between the leadership of business and of the self. He has intricately and skillfully woven multiple concepts, interspersed with personal stories, into processes to produce an integrated whole. I was very impressed to find that* The CEO Code *seamlessly encompasses business structures, values, ethics, human leadership with personal conscious awareness, empathy, emotional intelligence, processes, motivation with accountability and inspiration into a continuum of thorough treatment that could very well set a standard."*

—W. Michael King, PhD, BCC, advisor, mentor, board certified coach

"This book differs from most books for executives in that it explains the "how" to increase your and your employees effectiveness and improve relationships. The five communication practices, the execution procedures, and the leadership operations make this book a valuable investment."

—Dr. Marvin Marshall, author of *Discipline Without Stress*

"A CEO's job is the most difficult job in the world. David has cracked the code in a simple and elegant way. The CEO Code *provides key fundamentals for leading with a flair for developing the unique and artistic elements of leadership. I can say from personal experience that David truly cares about people, you, and has crafted an easy read that will make a difference in your leadership development."*

—Alan Rudi, general manager, Thesys International

"A terrific concept. Great advice from an executive who knows what really matters."

—Gene Griessman, PhD, author of *Time Tactics of Very Successful People* and *Lincoln on Communication*

"The CEO Code *is an important book. David's perspective is astute, current and timeless. Whether you are a new or experienced CEO you will find this book full of fresh new insights. If you want to increase profitability, gain an edge on competitors or master your unique competitive advantage you will want to read this book. Your competition will never know what hit them unless they read this book first.*"

—Pamela Stambaugh, president, AccountabilityPays

"*Mr. Rohlander's* The CEO Code *captures the essence of what not only a CEO, but also a CEO's direct reports, should use as management tools for success in dealing with issues and personnel on the path to creating a successful company. Like a well-organized legal brief, Mr. Rohlander's book is thought-provoking, laced with inspiring and persuasive quotes and clear and easy to read...a must for a CEO and his direct reports.*"

—Raymond F. Schuler, former vice president, secretary, and general counsel of three publicly traded multinational corporations, one a Fortune 500

"*If you follow David's advice and make good, new habits...make sure that one of them is reading this book—again and again.*"

—Jon Goodman, PhD, president, Town Hall Los Angeles

"*CEO (Communication, Execution and Operations) are the critical factors to success. David has done an excellent job of integrating the ways of success with the whys of competent action and on purpose thinking. His ability to take complex ideas and make them simple and applicable is a gift. Use the CEO to take your company to the next level. You and your organization will never be the same.*"

—Guy Baker, MBA, MSFS past president of The Million Dollar Round Table

"*David is the real deal, and his book is a must read for anyone—particularly lawyers like myself who seem to always need help with no nonsense business management!...—who either runs his own shop or aspires to do so. I've met lots of wannabe consultants and coaches, but too many follow formulaic patterns which ultimately don't work. David has a genuine love and passion for people and their organizations, and this comes through in this welcome new book.*"

—Dennis A. Stubblefield, attorney

THE
CEO
CODE

CREATE A GREAT COMPANY AND
INSPIRE PEOPLE TO GREATNESS WITH
PRACTICAL ADVICE FROM AN
EXPERIENCED EXECUTIVE

DAVID ROHLANDER

CAREER
PRESS
Pompton Plains, NJ

THE CEO CODE
EDITED BY ROGER SHEETY
TYPESET BY EILEEN MUNSON
Cover design by Ty Nowicki
Printed in the U.S.A.

To order this title, please call toll-free 1-800-CAREER-1 (NJ and Canada: 201-848-0310) to order using VISA or MasterCard, or for further information on books from Career Press.

CAREER
PRESS

The Career Press, Inc.
220 West Parkway, Unit 12
Pompton Plains, NJ 07444
www.careerpress.com

Library of Congress Cataloging-in-Publication Data

Rohlander, David, 1941-
  The CEO code : create a great company and inspire people to greatness with practical advice from an experienced executive / by David Rohlander.
      pages cm
  Includes bibliographical references and index.
  ISBN 978-1-60163-253-1 -- ISBN 978-1-60163-538-9 (ebook) 1. Chief executive officers. 2. Leadership. 3. Communication in management. 4. Personnel management. I. Title.
  HD38.2.R645 2013
  658.4'2--dc23
                                                          2012049263

Dedication

To Sixten
May he grow to love, laugh, and learn
as he creates his own masterpiece with gusto!

Acknowledgments

The most rewarding behavior I have found is to give to others without expecting to receive anything in return, to give merely to share blessings. As it says in the Bible, "It is more blessed to give than to receive." Fortunately, I have been the recipient of generosity and kindness for decades. I am very grateful. Here I wish to say thank you to the many people who have given so graciously of their time and wisdom.

To mention only a few that directly gave input to this book would be a mistake. The shaping and making of *The CEO Code* has been going on for decades. It is the interest and guidance of my grandmother when I was a small child, the people that educated me in schools, all the men and women I served with for this great country within the military, my clients, and colleagues. And today I even have the privilege of being taught by my son, Nathan, and his son, Sixten.

Life is a wonderful adventure; drink it up in full measure. Remember to pursue your goals with passion and enjoy the rewards in moderation. Then you will be able to say with me and Albert Camus, the Nobel Prize–winning author, journalist, and philosopher, "In the depth of winter, I finally learned that within me there lay an invincible summer."

CONTENTS

How Do People Really Change?

It ain't the roads we take; it's what's inside of us that makes us turn out the way we do.

—O. Henry

Frustration was in the air. Three executives and their driver were crammed into a small minivan. Stuck in heavy late afternoon traffic, they were going nowhere. Downtown Los Angeles is legendary for gridlock. Horns were blaring, and it was hot and stuffy in the van.

One of the executives, Andy, was the president of a major construction company. While Andy was riding shotgun, the other two executives sat in the back seat. The driver was doing his best but they were making no progress; the streets had turned into a parking lot. One of the executives in back checked his watch. "It's quarter till, we're going to be late," he proclaimed.

"Turn right in that alley," said Andy to the driver in a calm, measured voice. There was no traffic in the alley, just steep walls of concrete office buildings rising to block out the sky. The alley was narrow; they had to twist and turn to avoid trash bins as they maneuvered between the high-rise buildings. "After the next building, turn left." Andy was still calm and controlled as he gave instructions to the driver. The executives in the back seat were squeezed between boxes, a bit uneasy, and speechless.

They were driving in unknown territory. No traffic here but this back alley was dirty, dusty and full of piles of trash. "Follow this passageway for three blocks and then turn right," said Andy.

The driver did as he was told. Andy spoke with confidence; he was dressed to the nines, and at 6 feet 4 inches, a very impressive fellow. The executives in the back seat started to notice homeless people standing in the shadows, leaning against the buildings and sitting on cardboard. Driving in this part of the city was definitely making them uncomfortable.

Suddenly the dark alley began to get lighter; ahead they could see some sky and then, as if some huge doors were opened, they drove out of the maze and on to Main Street. Much to the surprise of the driver and the uneasy executives in the back, they arrived right in front of the Los Angeles Rescue Mission. Everyone in the van, except Andy, was surprised, impressed, and confused. One of the executives couldn't help himself: "How the hell did you do that Andy?"

Looking straight ahead, Andy replied in a matter-of-fact tone: "I lived on these streets for two and a half years when I was on the bottle. Fortunately, I hit bottom, decided to change, and worked my way back."

The company van was full of holiday food and gifts for the homeless of downtown Los Angeles. It was a few days before Christmas, and these executives were delivering gifts.

Change

There are many forms of change; as Heraclitus once said: "The only constant is change."[1] Simply put, people change in one of two ways. The first option is they have a significant emotional event and it becomes the catalyst for change. Classic examples of this are divorce, bankruptcy, heart attack, having a baby, inheriting a large sum of money, or falling in love. A few years ago, an obese attorney I know got divorced when his wife walked out. Divorce for him was a significant emotional event.

Today, having developed new eating and exercise behaviors, he is lean and running marathons. His whole life is changing and soon he will be getting married.

Some people choose not to change even after a significant emotional event. One CEO I know has had three heart attacks. Despite lengthy hospitalizations and rehabilitation, he is still a chain smoker. Significant emotional events did not cause him to change his habit.

The other fundamental way people change is they develop a personal insight and make a deliberate decision to create new behaviors. They then engage in a process of education, conditioning, and training to gradually develop and evolve.

The intent of this book is to help you avoid changing as the result of experiencing a significant emotional event. Rather, you will gain insight from *The CEO Code* that will stimulate you to embrace change and improvement. It is a guide to help you develop a plan and create your masterpiece.

Andy had a series of emotional events while living on the streets that, when added together, created so much pain he sought help and gradually turned his life around. Today he is a very successful business leader and enjoying a happy and healthy family life.

More than once I have met people who have a drinking, drug, or other addiction problem. When I questioned Andy about how to help them he consistently said that, from his point of view, they can't be helped until they hit the bottom. He bases that on his personal experience.

Everyone has a point of view. Their point of view is based on their own personal experience. One lesson I have learned over the years is that I am not always right, nor am I always wrong. Some people know they are always right, and from my experience I have learned to be very suspect of those people. Where do you fit? Have you assessed your point of view on how people change and, more importantly, how you change?

While reading this book you will have an opportunity to assess your beliefs, attitudes, and behaviors. A relevant theory developed by Julian Rotter in the 1950s is referred to as Locus of Control. "Locus" comes from the Latin word for *place* or *location*. "Control" relates to what individuals believe their life is controlled by, either internal or external factors. The two points of view are labeled Internal Locus of Control and External Locus of Control.

If you favor an internal locus of control you believe that your own behaviors and actions will influence your future outcomes and results. Those with an external locus of control believe that what happens to them is controlled by others, the environment or circumstances. Studies have shown that certain groups of people tend to lean one way or the other and have specific characteristics. Leaders tend to favor the internal locus of control and believe they have the power to make a difference. People who believe they are not able to control their circumstances have more anxiety and stress in their lives.

The CEO Code is a practical approach to growth and change. My clients are typically very successful executives yet they want to improve, to soar, and, as I like to say, "create a masterpiece." If you are like the majority of these high-achieving executives, you continually strive to improve your performance and your results. The ideas in this book are based on scientific research, years of business experience, and observation of what actually works in the real world. We have cracked the code.

Have you discovered the missing links that separate the average executive from the highest achievers? Did you ever ask yourself: What do they know that I don't? Is it luck or hard work? Is leadership learned or a genetic gift?

Natural talent is a wonderful thing to have, but far more success comes from learning what you need to do to improve yourself and hard work. Your journey to success and significance begins when you decide to learn all you can about how to change and ultimately make a commitment to do it. George Bernard Shaw once said, "The reasonable man adapts himself to the world; the unreasonable one persists in trying to adapt the world to himself. Therefore, all progress depends on the unreasonable man."[2]

The CEO Code identifies and clarifies the knowledge, attitudes, skills, and behaviors necessary to become a great leader and inspire your people to greatness. Talent helps, but the most important ingredient is what you are able to learn and practice so you will improve. Our goal is mastery.

We will focus on three critical areas. First and most important is **communication**. Authentic communication is required to build a team and company that runs smoothly and is productive. Peter Drucker often shared a simple metaphor: Communication is the oil that keeps the machine we call business running smoothly.

Execution is next. Timeliness, precision, and competence when demonstrated in the execution of your strategy and tasks will determine a productive outcome. You will be learning several methods and techniques to help you execute and ensure that you and your team are ready and able to do so.

Operations is the third area. Operations includes designing systems to help teams function and methods to monitor and implement delegation effectively. I will share solutions to help you design accountability and rewards so your people are enthusiastic and committed to working together at peak performance levels.

Isn't it time for some courageous and creative decision-making? Are you ready to break through to the next level and create better tangible results? *The CEO Code* will help you create a great company and inspire your people to greatness with proven, practical advice that works. Let's get started.

PART I

COMMUNICATION

Effective communication takes more than talent. It requires trust, respect, understanding, empathy, and resolution. It is an art. Many elements are under the broad umbrella we call communication. How a leader needs to communicate with his or her people is our focus. Communication is by definition a two-way process, a form of conversation or dialogue.

Popular opinion has a tendency to think communication is mostly about talking and writing, or what we might call "broadcasting." This is a very limiting perspective. Broadcast brings to mind monikers like: The Great Communicator or The Consummate Speaker, and individuals such as Franklin D. Roosevelt, Ronald Reagan, or Martin Luther King.

Half or more of the communication equation is the "receiving" of information. Being able to read or understand what others are trying to say or relate takes effort. We need to connect with people on a personal basis. Standing on a podium or using a teleprompter or microphone does not help develop relationships or dialogue.

Dan, VP of sales and marketing, was encouraged to get some coaching by his CEO. This VP was under a lot of pressure to produce, was extremely overweight, and yet was very talented. The boss didn't want to lose him. As is customary, the CEO shared several concerns with me before my first meeting with the VP.

Dan and I met for our first meeting in a small conference room. It was an opportunity to get acquainted, share expectations, and agree on a format and agenda. Dan was very charming, clearly intelligent, and focused on doing a stellar job at the company. After sharing a brief introduction and overview I started to ask a few questions, simple at first: Where did you go to school, what jobs have you had, how about your goals?

He was very open and gregarious. He told me about his background, his past job experiences, and really got animated when he started telling me about his kids. The conversation went on for a good half hour and I was mainly in listener mode.

Finally there was a comfortable pause. I looked him straight in the eye, and very slowly and softly asked a simple question: "Dan, are you married?" There was silence. He blinked, turned his head and his eyes, and then looked down. I could see tension building in his neck. After a bit, I gently said, "You haven't mentioned a wife."

At this point, he broke down. His eyes welled up with tears and he said, "I didn't want to go there. We are having some real serious problems."

What Dan did not want to talk about was his most significant, urgent, and emotional issue.

It is impossible not to communicate. Even when you choose to be silent, you are communicating. One of the keys to effective listening is to be tuned to what is not being said. This often is more revealing than what is said.

There are many obvious techniques to use while broadcasting or receiving. There are also many nuances to learn. Communication is absolutely critical for you to master for success in your personal life and your professional life. In the next five chapters we will delve deeply into how you can become a great communicator. We're talking about a lot more than just being a "good talker."

Chapter 1

TRUST

Trust must be earned. Fundamentally, people trust each other when they do what they say they will do. All too often trust is lost when there is a difference between what a person says and what they actually do. This can be illustrated in numerous ways.

When you say you will be at work at 8 a.m. and you don't show up until 8:30 a.m., your behavior belies what you say. If you say you will call someone and you don't, people will hesitate to believe you in the future. You say you care; you express concern and say you want to help someone, and then you never follow up. What do you think others will conclude? Any promise you make that is not honored will compromise trust. This may seem simplistic, but people notice and remember these behaviors. They may not say anything, but they will remember.

People make judgments about other people based on small—what many consider to be trivial—things. They also observe nuances of behavior. They perceive someone with "shifty eyes," a "glib tongue," or inconsistent patterns of behavior as not being trustworthy. The ultimate litmus test is based on behavior, not who you know, what you say, or how smart you are.

Competence

Nothing in my personal or business life has even come close to the trust relationship I experienced flying fighters in formation. When I reflect on my military combat experience, there are many lessons that are useful and apply directly to civilian life and business.

The qualifications to be a United States Air Force pilot are rigorous. When you fly fighters, you have to meet all the basic pilot requirements, plus you must be proficient in flying formation. That means you fly a few feet away from another aircraft, sometimes close to the ground, sometimes in the clouds, and sometimes in beautiful blue skies. There is always a lead, and the rest are wingmen. As a wingman, you follow lead, and where lead goes, you go.

The first two critical factors for fighter pilots in formation flying are competence and good judgment. In combat, lack of competence or poor decision-making can result in not only your own demise, but also the death of your wingman.

When I graduated from pilot training I was able to fly very precisely. I consistently pegged the altitude, heading, and airspeed. However, being a good fighter pilot requires a lot more than simple precision flying. After flying a couple of years and having logged 208 combat missions, I was a much better pilot, and had better judgment and high competence. Flying the airplane was almost automatic, and the mission or hitting the target was my primary focus. The airplane became an extension of my own body.

My squadron in Vietnam lost several aircrews and aircraft. On more than one occasion, I was assigned to investigate aircraft losses, and brief the general on what happened and what we could do to avoid the same mistake again by another aircrew. Gradually it became apparent that there were patterns of behavior, some good and some bad, that became habits by the pilots. Some planned very thoroughly, others had a tendency to take high-risk chances, and unfortunately all pilots are not equally gifted with superior skills.

One of the biggest lessons I learned is that usually it is not one mistake that causes you to crash or get shot down. It is multiple things that happen at the same time. It might be a combination of poor weather, not being at your peak physically, and a slip-up in communications. Having an engine problem is usually manageable, but if and when it is combined with all these other problems, you are suddenly at great risk. You may crash, and if you are flying over enemy territory, it may result in getting shot down.

It's exactly the same in business. The good news for businesspeople is that it usually is not your life in the balance, like it would be in combat. Let's look at a simple example. Maybe the economy is plagued with high unemployment, lack of consumer confidence, and confused leadership in Washington, DC. Interest rates are at an all-time low, but new regulations make it almost impossible to get your clients financing. You feel stressed and decide you need a break.

You stay out late dwelling too much on the downward spiraling economy, have that extra glass of wine, and get a slow start in the morning. On the way to the office, because you are rushing and running late, you decide to text someone while you are driving: "I'm on my way."

The reality is that this scenario could turn into a ticket, a car accident, or just getting stuck in heavy traffic. However, the bottom line is you said you would be at work before 8 a.m. It's now 8:30 a.m. and you are late. How would you handle this minor situation? Would you cruise into the office trying to put on a charming smile? What do you say? Do you ignore the fact that you are late? Maybe you are clever, and you make a joke about your car or traffic? How about a very humble apology? But more importantly, you may now have created a complex problem. What is the fundamental problem—the real issue? What has happened to *trust*?

When you have been in business a long time, several decades in my case, you have the opportunity to observe people in many situations with both good and bad outcomes. This gives the experienced person an advantage. It is the ability to recognize patterns. Let me share a few of the patterns I have seen over the years that relate to the simple story I just told about getting to work a half hour late.

Anyone who is often late has a problem. Obviously, the habit of being late destroys trust. However, the root of the problem may relate to self-concept. Sometimes the person believes his or her time is more valuable than another person's time. But even more telling is how this behavior relates to respect. (Chapter 2 is an in-depth discussion of respect.)

Another issue may be a person's inability to make good decisions. Some people try to pack too much into the time they have. This is commonly known as "being behind the power curve." This expression relates to flying. When you get behind the power curve, your aircraft will lose altitude or stall, no matter how hard you pull back on the stick and try to climb. There simply is not enough power to overcome the weight and drag of the aircraft. The solution in flying is to let up on the stick, push the nose down, and let the aircraft build up speed without the pressure of trying to climb. This goes against natural instinct, especially if you are close to or approaching the ground. In business, when you are caught behind the power curve, you need to take a deep breath, assess the reality of the situation, and reduce your commitments. Ease up on the stick. When people are is not able to manage themselves within time frames, they are considered unreliable. It is a competency issue that will destroy trust.

Good Judgment

Knowing how to make decisions using good judgment is a learned skill. It is valuable to spend time with more experienced people when you are striving to develop the discernment necessary to have good judgment. The simple truth is there is no substitute for experience.

People have a tendency to trust others if they have "been there and done that." That's why the American pioneers would hire a scout to get them across Indian Territory. Today modern business leaders hire mentors and coaches to work with their fast-track managers. The goal is to improve managers' competence at an accelerated rate. Increased understanding will reduce mistakes and build a more complete tool kit for the manager. Mentoring and coaching, when combined with experience, will improve their judgment.

We all make mistakes, and they can be very costly in business. They can also ruin a firm's reputation. However, mistakes can be a great learning tool. Ideally a firm's culture will embrace mistakes and convert them into learning opportunities. It takes good judgment to know how to balance learning from mistakes versus a lack of tolerance for incompetence.

Training is a good way to help people overcome these behavioral shortcomings. Years after my Air Force experience I was introduced to Boots Boothby, a former fighter pilot and retired Air Force Lieutenant Colonel. Boots was a few years ahead of me in Vietnam. After the war, he was commissioned by the Pentagon to analyze why our air combat results had deteriorated when compared to the stellar results we had in Korea.

As a result of his research, he was able to persuade the Air Force to start an aggressor squadron. This group was designed to give pilots actual flying practice against the tactics used by the enemy. You may remember the movie *Top Gun*. Well, according to Boots, that movie was based on the USAF aggressor squadron he helped create at Nellis Air Force Base in Nevada. When the movie script was completed, the producers were unable to get approval from the USAF generals. The producers then took the script, reworked it, and offered it to the U.S. Navy. They loved it. Smart move by the Navy—it was great public relations and really helped with recruiting.

The United States has dramatically improved air combat results in the several conflicts that have been fought since we were fighting in Southeast Asia. This positive result is directly attributable to the intensive and experiential air combat training provided by both the Air Force and the Navy in their respective programs. Training works in business, too.

Several years ago, Honeywell was having a significant problem in their Western Region. The results were miserable. They were at 70 percent of their forecasted sales. A new regional manager was brought in to turn the situation around. One of my sales reps happened to call on him soon after he arrived in Orange County. She asked me to join her on the second meeting, and he and I hit it off. He was a graduate of the U.S. Air Force Academy and a former fighter pilot.

We worked with his entire sales team for several months. The training included workshops and lesson manuals; back then, we used audio tapes to reinforce the principles. However, the most important parts of the training were going out with the sales reps on sales calls, helping them craft their presentations, and giving them feedback on their performance. In less than eight months, the region was at more than 200 percent of the sales forecast. Intensive and experiential training works. It improves the ability of executives to make good decisions. The improved judgment helps build trust.

Confidentiality

Trust is a primary ingredient required to open a sincere dialogue. When you trust another person, you are more sincere, because you are not inhibited with fear or concern for your own welfare or safety. You are able to be open and honest.

This does not mean that if you trust someone there is no longer a need to think before you speak. There are times when it is best to refrain from full disclosure. In the military, there is a guideline for disclosing information: An individual must have a *need to know* classified information. That need relates to what is required to successfully accomplish the mission.

One of the easiest ways for a leader to destroy trust is to openly share information that is not necessary to accomplish a mission. You have probably seen this happen with political leaders who have compromised sensitive information. It soon becomes clear that their intent is to enhance their own image or to get re-elected at the expense of others. Trust will also be compromised when someone is sloppy or undisciplined with confidential or sensitive information. When people are loose with confidential or personal information, it causes resentment, anxiety, and a conscious guardedness on the part of employees or political operatives.

Trust is earned when you honor others. The opposite of this is exhibited when people gossip. People that are aware realize that if a person is prone to gossiping about someone to them, the individual will probably not hesitate to also gossip about them when given the opportunity. This will compromise trust.

Connie Chung, an established news reporter, gained notoriety in 1995 when she asked the mother of a politician to whisper what her son, a politician, really thought of another politician. The elderly woman whispered a response in Connie's ear. The answer was then broadcast on the network, and the fiery commentaries started. Trust is very hard to earn and can easily be lost with one fatal mistake.

Self–Discipline

Self-discipline is a basic requirement to building trust. You must be aware of what you are communicating, and why you are sharing or receiving information. Every contact and exchange you have with another person provides an opportunity to build or diminish trust. People are always watching you.

Self-discipline is exercised when you listen well to another person. It has been said that good listening is a platonic form of making love. When you actively listen to someone and you actually hesitate or refrain from speaking, it gives the person talking the joy of expressing him- or herself, as well as the time to reflect on what and how he or she is saying something. Quality listening takes a conversation to a much deeper level. It also tends to remove anxiety and provides calm and comfort to the person talking.

This level of listening needs to be totally nonjudgmental, even in your nonverbal cues. You must remember that there are many ways to communicate besides talking. You can show disdain or judgment by simply raising your eyebrow. That simple reaction will prompt the person you are with to withdraw or possibly even have an emotional reaction.

When my son was in fourth grade, I started developing the habit of spending time with him alone. There was no agenda—just time together. Sometimes we'd go out to breakfast together, I'd teach him woodworking, or we would just take a long car trip—an absolutely wonderful habit that we still enjoy, though he is now approaching 40 years old! One of the most important keys in our times together is to listen and not be judgmental. It is not easy, but you can learn how to do it. My reward is that today my son and I are best friends.

Intention

Watch what a person pays attention to, and you can tell what his or her unconscious intention is. A few years ago I heard a high-ranking official from the Central Intelligence Agency say in a television interview that it is hard for someone to judge another's intention, so we have to work backward from action. This is how the CIA attempts to determine what the intentions of various countries are. It is not easy.

Leaders in organizations have the same dilemma; they are continually striving to decipher the intentions of their people, their competition, and policy makers in government. We all know that actions are much more reliable than words. This is demonstrated every day on television by the politicians trying to persuade people to vote for them over their rival. How often do they do what they say they will do? Do you trust them?

In the process of coaching, it is critical to understand the difference between what people say and what they do. You have to learn how to do the same thing. I would recommend that you spend some high-quality time and effort to become a student of people.

A considerable part of this book will deal with *how* to relate to people. I will share insights on how to read people as part of the understanding required for effective leadership and communication in Chapter 3.

The CIA is tasked to go to places and do things that are uncomfortable and potentially dangerous. This is the core of how we achieve the requisite intelligence to defend our country and our way of life. You need to approach your business and personal life in the same manner if you wish to achieve great things. You must push your comfort zone.

Open Honesty

Not long ago there was a glut of investment money available. A large venture capital firm purchased an aerospace manufacturing firm in Southern California and brought in a new CEO to fix it. During his second week on the job, a scruffy-looking fellow walked into his office unannounced. This uninhibited visitor had obviously been there before; he was familiar with the office, but he was surprised to see its new occupant. He was looking for the former CEO.

The new CEO asked him who he was. "I'm with XYZ company, and we pick up and get rid of your trash and waste metal."

"How can I help you?" said the new CEO.

"Gee, I'm not sure," he said. "If Joe is gone and you're the new owner, I guess this is for you."

He then handed him a rather large roll of cash.

The new CEO soon found out that this was just the tip of the iceberg; there was more corruption. This firm had acquired many accounts by providing illicit services for clients—in addition to the heavy drinking and parties.

The sale of the company to the venture capital firm had shocked most of the employees. They were all a bit scared, confused, and nervous about the future. To stay with the company, some had done things that compromised good business ethics and sometimes the law. Several had hired relatives in their departments. Of the 15 people in purchasing, 12 of them were related. Evaluations were based on things other than productive performance.

Hard to believe, I know, but it is true. The previous CEO had several flaws, including a drinking problem. When a leader or anyone has character issues, it will destroy trust throughout the entire organization. The new CEO had lots of work to do to turn the company around.

One of the first things the new CEO did was to bring me in to help. I started talking to people about how and what they were doing. We implemented several seminars and workshops designed to pull the team together and improve productivity. Several times we had very emotional meetings. People wanted to get the truth out, but they had been conditioned to keep secrets. They were afraid for their own jobs.

Probably one of the smartest things the new CEO did was start an "open door" policy. His version of that was walking around and getting to know people, but also inviting anyone and everyone to stop by his office after 4 p.m. to talk; there was no agenda. He let them know that he would stay as late as necessary if they wanted to chat. Many nights he didn't leave the office until 8 or 9 p.m.

The result was that, in time, people came forward and shared concerns. This built rapport and ultimately trust was developed. The CEO was then able to share his concerns for the company with key employees, as well as learn more about the individual employees and how they could best develop in the future. As time went by, they developed confidence and were able to share openly. Mutual sharing led to understanding, and people got to know each other at a deeper level. Gradually, they were able to rely on the veracity of what was shared. This became a very positive and healing process.

The CEO also shared, in writing, his code of conduct. Because this CEO actually lived by this code, it was very effective. Throughout history, significant leaders have done similar things.

George Washington is noted for having written a Rules of Civility and Behavior when his teacher wanted him to develop his penmanship as a young student. Historians believe these rules influenced his character and behavior as the first leader of a new nation, the United States of America. These rules were originally developed by Jesuit Instructors in the 16th century. "Associate yourself with men of good quality if you esteem your own reputation; for 'tis better to be alone than in bad company"[1] was one of them.

Benjamin Franklin had his own rules of conduct, such as, "I will never speak ill of anybody."[2] He also identified 13 virtues that he wrote down on a list and carried in his pocket so he would remember to work on them. Even Mother Teresa had some rules to live by: "If you are honest and frank, people may cheat you. Be honest and frank anyway."[3]

Developing Trust

Intuitively, people are a lot more aware of others than most realize. They may not be formally trained on how to develop trust, but they know who they trust and who they don't. Conversely, many highly educated people have a distinct deficit in their ability to relate to people.

You can master several simple disciplines to enhance trust. The beauty of these disciplines is that they will change who you are as you develop them. That change will create a positive result.

First and foremost, you need to develop competence in your chosen field. There is no easy way to do this. It takes study, training, and hard work. When you develop competence, you also develop self-confidence, which is the first prerequisite of being a leader. You will have aptitude in your field, and it will be obvious to those who are watching you. You will not have to tell people how great you are; it will be apparent.

Second, you must have good judgment. There is no substitute for experience when you are learning how to make good decisions. One thing to remember is that we learn more from our mistakes than we do from our successes. Periodically, you need to review your interpersonal performance and analyze what the lesson is from each good and bad experience. Seeking the assistance of a mentor or coach can dramatically enhance this process.

Confidentiality is absolutely necessary to establish a trusting relationship. One of the best ways for you to learn this is to develop the habit of asking yourself the Four-Way Test of Rotary International:

- ▶ Is it the truth?
- ▶ Is it fair to all concerned?
- ▶ Will it build goodwill and better friendships?
- ▶ Will it be beneficial to all concerned?

Before you speak or act, hesitate and take the time to think of the other person. What will be the impact of your words and actions? When people see that you take them into consideration and are concerned about them, it enables them to trust you. Because it is intuitive to observe people and get a sense as to what they care about, we easily identify those who are totally self-centered and not focused on the greater good.

Demonstrating self-discipline in your communication is most obvious by your ability to listen more than you speak. It is a very high compliment when you give another person your undivided attention. There is no single thing you can do that is more valuable in developing trust.

Everyone has an agenda. People will determine your agenda by what you say and especially by what you do. It is a very worthwhile use of your time to clarify, in writing, what your agenda is. This has everything to do with your vision and mission for your life. When you clarify this simple concept, memorialize it in writing, and start to live life on a daily basis that is consistent with it, you will have clarity of intention.

When in doubt, be open and honest. Honesty truly is the best policy. I cannot tell you how many times people have gotten into difficult, tight, or simply embarrassing situations because they were false and loose with the truth. You will see as you read this book that many of the very complex problems people have created boil down to violation of these simple principles.

If you are at all like me, you don't have enough time to make all the mistakes yourself. Let's learn from each other's mistakes. You will then make more money, have more fun, and create a great company.

Take Time to Reflect

As you contemplate this chapter take a few minutes alone and answer these questions.

1. What behaviors do you consistently do that instill trust?

2. How are you deliberately working to improve your competence? In what areas?

3. Do people ever comment on or compliment you for good judgment?

4. Are you known as a person who keeps someone's sensitive information confidential?

5. How often do people thank you for listening well?

6. Are your intentions transparent or do you have a hidden agenda?

7. What specific evidence do you have that people trust you?

Chapter 2

RESPECT

A great man shows his greatness by the way he treats little men.

—Thomas Carlyle

If your intention is to communicate effectively with someone, it is necessary for you to have respect for that person. Many would argue that respect is earned and that not everyone deserves respect. A person is entitled to hold this point of view. However, as long as that is their perspective, they will have difficulty communicating with others.

Recently, the president of the United States was interrupted by a reporter in the middle of a sentence during a news conference in the Rose Garden of the White House. This behavior demonstrates a total lack of respect for the office, as well for as the individual holding that office. News commentators reacted strongly based on their political orientation, either for or against the president. Others were concerned because lack of civility has become commonplace in our country. No matter how you view it, the net result was a negative impact on effective communication between the two individuals, as well as the general population of the country.

Lack of respect in our daily lives can be a lot more subtle than this example. I am reminded of the time I was meeting a CEO client in his office, and we decided to break for lunch at a restaurant. The company was in severe financial straits, and the week before there was a major layoff. As we were walking through the lobby, the CEO was chatting away, excited to show me his new sports car parked out front. I nodded to the receptionist, smiled, and did a little wave with my right hand. She was new to the office, and I had not seen her before.

I asked the CEO, as we approached his new car, what the new receptionist's name was. Giving the question little attention and with a flip of his hand he said, "I don't know." And then, as we reached the car, with a bit of enthusiasm he said, "Let me open the door so you can see the interior. Isn't it a beauty?" Hopefully, you would not behave the way the reporter or the CEO did.

What Is Respect?

The dictionary definition of *respect* relates to admiration, having regard for another, and practicing various elements of etiquette. Otis Redding and Aretha Franklin sing a song about R-E-S-P-E-C-T, one of the most popular songs ever recorded. The military trains recruits to automatically say "Sir" and "Ma'am," and to honor the hierarchy of ranks with a salute to any superior officer. Everyone has a slight variation on exactly what they mean by respect.

Effective communication between two people requires respect and is all about honoring the other person. You can honor others and show respect in many ways, but the best way is to master the art of listening. You have heard it said that when God designed man and woman he very deliberately gave us one mouth, two ears, and two eyes. The mouth is for talking, and the ears and eyes for listening. Because we have only one mouth, we should do half as much talking as we do listening.

Respect is demonstrated more by how we behave than what we say. Glib salesmen, politicians, and hucksters may say all kinds of flattering things. They are trying to compliment you, so you will think they care about you. Have you ever had a salesperson share how impressed he or she is by your clothes, jewelry, or intelligence? The salesperson who notices the trophy on the shelf or fish on the wall may quickly share his or her own interest in the sport or fishing.

I know a clever communication speaker who tells a funny story about one of her first sales in her first year out of college. She just happened to see a show about bass fishing while channel surfing on TV. A day or two later, she was in an executive's office trying to sell her services, and she noticed a fish on the wall. Fortunately, she remembered the name of the TV show and combined that with her charm and a smile, as they say, the rest of the story is history. She made a big sale.

But it's not just salespeople. Politicians are notorious for using surveys and polls to determine what should be said in the next town or state to garner the most votes. Hucksters come in many varieties. The most common in our popular culture are the car salesperson and the person who works in money products and services (insurance, stocks and bonds, mortgages, title insurance, and real estate). And of course, you probably have your own stories about attorneys.

Stop; let's hold on a minute. Can all those professions be that bad? No, they are not. The real point is, it's not *what* you do for a living. What really matters is *how you do it*. There are many honorable people in each and every one of the professions I just listed. Unfortunately, if you or I have a severe negative emotional experience with someone in any profession, we have a tendency to castigate their entire industry. It's what might be called a "meltdown" or an "intense reaction." (I will explain why we react this way later in this book.)

Totally normal and knowledgeable people may be a bit suspect or cautious when they are communicating with others. Everyone has been burned at one time or another. People routinely make associations and conclusions based on their past experience with certain types of people. When you meet someone, an assessment is made in a matter of seconds that is either positive or negative. Some people you like, and others you are uncomfortable with before they say a word. This judgment happens almost instantly, and it is intuitive.

You don't need a college education to know when someone is arrogant or full of hubris. You can tell by the way he holds his head and nose a little up in the air, or by the way she glances out of the side of her eye rather than directly at you. He might even turn his shoulders away from you and walk toward another person. When you see this behavior, it does not lead to effective communication. Instead, you might possibly think that person doesn't respect you.

How you behave toward other people is a manifestation of the respect you have for them. When you focus on other's concerns, ideas, and situation in a nonjudgmental way, you are showing them respect. By being aware of their point of view and behaving in a way to honor them even when you disagree with them, you are showing them respect. This does not mean that you compromise who you are or what your values are, or that you give up on pursuing your own agenda.

Pablo Rivera

Several years ago I did some major work around the house. I really enjoy working with wood, building things, and working on the garden. I needed some help, so I decided to hire someone. Pablo Rivera was referred to me by a neighbor.

Pablo was just over 5 feet tall and a lot shorter than me; I'm 6'2". I never saw him without his white cowboy hat, and he always showed up early for work. He knew all about horses, cattle, and farming. He worked very hard, he loved his family, and he was also a proud man.

We worked well together. When we had to dig a hole, he'd pick and I would shovel for a while, then we would switch, and I would pick and he would shovel. At one point, we dug a beautiful koi pond and Jacuzzi about 6 feet deep, all by hand. Pablo wasn't too familiar with some of the power tools I have, but he learned quickly how to use them.

Midway through this major project, it was time to build a retaining wall with a cinder block base. A masonry contractor was hired to build the block wall. Pablo worked with the contractor's men; he actually worked harder than they did. Their rude and dismissive behavior made it obvious they did not have high regard for Pablo. They didn't respect him. After lunch, I had seen enough. I wrote a check and asked the contractor to pick up his spade and his men and leave. "Adios." Pablo and I finished the job.

Pablo spoke no English and I don't speak Spanish; yet after a hard day's work we would sit on the porch, I would get him and myself a cerveza (beer), and we would talk by using lots of sign language and the few words we taught each other.

This working relationship went on for a few years. Along the way, my family was invited to his granddaughter's christening, and we joined his family for the reception afterward. He personally made the mole sauce, and it was delicious.

Nathan, my son, is an artist, and one day while visiting, he asked if he could paint Pablo's portrait. Pablo wanted to get to work and didn't understand what we were asking him to do. Finally, we were able to explain what we wanted to do. It took a couple of hours and turned out really well. The painting is now used in my presentations as an illustration of *respect*. By the way, Pablo enjoyed getting paid that day for sitting on a stool.

A few months later, Pablo approached me in the garage. He just stood there looking down. Then he took a step forward and put his arms around me. His white cowboy hat was below my chin and pressing into my chest. As we stood there I could feel him shaking as he said, "Adios, Patron. Adios."

Pablo moved back to Mexico, where he owned a ranch. I respected Pablo and he respected me. It was obvious to both of us, because of the way we behaved and treated each other. The primary basis of the relationship was hard work and compensation. It began as strictly business yet, through time, we became great friends. As Aristotle says, "Wishing to be friends is quick work, but friendship is a slow ripening fruit."[1]

Where does respect come from?

So, what is the easy answer? Are there any tricks or a few simple things you can do to receive and give respect? Well, unfortunately the answer is no. Respect takes a lot more than just saying "yes, sir" to your elders. It's more involved than that.

It really starts with your self-concept. For centuries, philosophers and religions of the world have given guidance to their followers about self-love, how to treat others, and how to behave. Only you know who you really are and what your self-concept is.

Please put on your thinking cap and review these historical quotes from various cultures as you contemplate your self-concept.

- ▶ "Respect yourself and others will respect you."
  —Confucius[2]

- ▶ "And walk not on the earth with conceit and arrogance."
  —al-Isra' 17:37[3]

- ▶ "And turn not your face away from men with pride."
  —Luqmaan 31:18[4]

- ▶ "Peace comes from within. Do not seek it without."
  —Hindu Prince Gautama Siddharta, founder of Buddhism, 563–483 BC[5]

▶ "You yourself, as much as anybody in the entire universe, deserve your love and affection."
—Gautama Siddharta[6]

▶ "You shall love your neighbor as yourself."
—Matthew 22:39[7]

▶ "Instead of being motivated by selfish ambition or vanity, each of you should, in humility, be moved to treat one another as more important than yourself."
—Philippians 2:3[8]

▶ "Remember that the best relationship is one in which your love for each other exceeds your need for each other."
—Dalai Lama XIV[9]

▶ "When you are content to be simply yourself and don't compare or compete, everyone will respect you."
—Lao Tzu[10]

▶ "It is necessary to the happiness of man that he be mentally faithful to himself."
—Thomas Paine[11]

Your self-concept is the beginning of being able to respect another person. If you don't respect yourself, you will not be able to respect another. The Golden Rule says to "Treat others as you would like to be treated. However, there is a better rule for you to consider. That better way is the Platinum Rule: Treat others the way *they* want to be treated. This means you have to understand the difference in each individual and be able to respond to them based on their individual preferences and needs. This is discussed at length in the next chapter.

One of the best ways to achieve clarity is the process of writing. Take a few minutes and write down, as a first draft or working document, exactly what you believe your self-concept is. Clearly understanding "self" is a first step as you create a masterpiece of your personal life. This is very simple to do. However, it may not be easy. Trust me; it is well worth the effort. Do it now.

What about the other guy?

Once you have a clear understanding of who you are, what your values are, and how you choose to behave, it is time to focus on the other person. If you are concerned about developing quality communication, it is imperative that you demonstrate respect for others. The catch here is that you need to respect everyone, not just those people who are smarter, richer, or more famous than you, and not only those who are in a position to help you advance in your career or business. Try it. You will be amazed at the reaction you get when you sincerely respect and politely acknowledge others—everyone.

There are two very Machiavellian reasons why this should be important to you. One is that people are watching you all the time, and they will sometimes make unfounded conclusions.

They may think that if you don't respect people of lesser station or talents, that you probably have some personal "issues." Yes, many people think they are qualified psychologists, and they make assumptions. Your observers may think things like "He acts that way because he is so short; he's got a Napoleon complex," or "She didn't earn her new job based on merit and now she thinks she's special," or "The reason he is so abrupt is that he really is very insecure and afraid someone else may have a better idea." If this concept is new to you, read Dale Carnegie's book, *How to Win Friends and Influence People*.

The other Machiavellian reason is that you don't want to be caught in the uncomfortable situation of meeting someone on your way down the ladder of success that you stepped on while on your way up the same ladder. A far better reason to show respect for everyone is based on wisdom from people who have lived productive lives many years ago and done things we just dream about.

Aristotle once said, "Democracy arises out of the notion that those who are equal in any respect are equal in all respects; because men are equally free, they claim to be absolutely equal."[12] Notice that Aristotle says they "claim" to be absolutely equal. This directly relates to the Declaration of Independence of the United States which says: "We hold these truths to be self-evident, that all men are created equal, that they are endowed by their Creator with certain unalienable Rights, that among these are Life, Liberty and the pursuit of Happiness."[13] Given this claim on rights, you can make a good case for the principle that all men and women have an equal right to claim respect. When you choose to give respect to another person, you will find it dramatically improves your communication with that person.

You may agree or disagree with the idea of people having a right to claim respect. You may also argue that certain behaviors by an individual necessitate a forfeiture of respect. Be careful, when you take either of these views, that everything you say and do is above reproach, and your motives or intentions are pure. The only person that you are able to totally control is yourself. It reminds me of what Jesus said to the religious leaders who caught a woman in adultery: "Let him who is without sin, throw the first stone."[14]

How Do You Do It?

Giving respect can be done in many ways; some are obvious and others are very subtle. The more obvious ways we see in specific behaviors. It is just a matter of having regard for the other person's comfort by, for example, holding a chair, opening a door, and removing your hat indoors or when talking to another person. Try standing up when someone approaches you, or being gracious enough to ask if you may get the person a water or coffee. It is rewarding when you offer someone your seat, allow a person to go ahead in line, or actually let another driver go first in a tight traffic situation.

Undoubtedly, you know how to be introduced and to introduce others: firm handshake, eye contact, and a pleasant greeting. However, in a communications situation involving intimate dialogue, showing respect may be more subtle. When you are with someone, do you consciously give the other person time and space to talk more than you? A professional salesperson knows that it is critical to ask questions and do a lot of listening. In fact, respect is, in reality, an attempt to sell yourself to the other person. I am continually amazed how many people think this means talking about yourself as opposed to listening.

The real mastery comes when you are able to make it look natural and easy to show respect. You are so real that the other person is simply thrilled just to be with you. By showing respect, you are showing him or her how much you care. Do you often get e-mails or phone calls after you have met with people telling you how delightful it was just to be with you?

The language you use is a reflection of how much you respect yourself and others. Do you speak politely and use proper English? Do you swear, curse, or use crude language in front of others? How about your humor? Is it appropriate, clean, and high class? Hopefully you don't gossip. You see, people know that if you gossip about other people *to* them, they can be certain you will also gossip to others *about* them. It's a quick and easy way to destroy respect.

Are you both "interesting" and "interested"? A person is interesting when he or she has a broad palette of knowledge and experience that also has depth. She is interested when she listens and asks good questions. One becomes charming when the primary focus and amount of time is mostly on the other person.

You must also be able to appropriately reveal information about yourself in a conversation or relationship. We call this self-disclosure. Learning to be measured with the amount of self disclosure, and adapting this to different people is an art form. It takes time and practice. Respect is evident when you minimize self.

Respect and Power

Power is a real and necessary part of all relationships. Power is much like money, in that both can be used for good or evil. The choice is yours and is dependent upon your personal values. There are many forms of power; let's briefly review a few. John French and Bertram Raven developed a useful model for power back in 1959. Our discussion is based on their views, as well as the work since the 1960s of many people, including Paul Hersey at the Center for Leadership Studies. Dr. Hersey is the originator of Situational Leadership, which he considers to be merely common sense. He also believes that leadership is simply influence. Power is one of the ways we influence others, and everyone has one or more forms of power.

Power can derive from a person's position or personal attributes. Legitimate or positional power comes from the title, position, or rank a person has in an organization. Then there are two other types or groups of power; one group is based on personal attributes, while the other is often referred to as formal or organizational power.

Formal power may be broken into several areas that include reward power, connection power, and coercive power. Reward power is the ability to influence, control, or bestow rewards upon others. This may be as elementary as assigning parking spots or determining annual bonuses. Connection power usually has political, family, or special relationships that provide the source of the power. It can be referred to as the "good old boy network," the fraternity connection, or simply knowing people well because of your work group or discipline within a company. The last is coercive power. This is well discussed in Machiavelli's *The Prince*. As the word *coercive* implies, it is the dark side of influencing people to do what you want them to do: "I've got a deal you can't refuse."

The personal power group is unique because you can control and develop personal power if you are willing to work smart and hard. Expert power is bestowed on someone who has demonstrated his or her ability, knowledge, and expertise in a particular field. This can be developed by schooling, training, and experience. You totally control how much of an expert you wish to become. The more you know about a specific topic or field, the more expert power you have.

Information power is closely aligned to expert power. The difference is the person with informational power simply knows the who, what, why, where, and how of the operation, the market, or the field. A person with information power has a much broader focus than the expert. Often an employee who has been in an organization for a long period of time will accumulate informational power. Again, it takes hard work, plus a keen sense of awareness, to develop informational power.

Referent power is the last and, in my view, most important type of power. Referent power refers to the ability of a leader to influence a follower because of the follower's loyalty, respect, friendship, admiration, affection, or a desire to gain approval from the leader. The only way to acquire referent power is by being a person of the highest character and consistently behaving with integrity. People will notice your behavior, and you will never have to ask for respect. It will be gladly given to you by your followers. As Margaret Thatcher put it, "Being powerful is like being a lady. If you have to tell people you are, you aren't."[15]

Take Time to Reflect

As you contemplate this chapter take a few minutes alone and answer these questions.

1. How often do people ask you for your opinion, and then listen or take notes?

2. What kind of comments and feedback, if any, do you get from time spent with others?

3. How well do you know your people (details such as their names, goals, fears, talents, needs, and concerns)?

4. Do you have a personal mission statement that is written and that you reviewed regularly?

5. Who do you respect and why? Who do you not respect and why?

6. Given that your behavior influences others, is it consistent with your values?

7. Examine your power and how you currently use it. Is there room for improvement?

Chapter 3

UNDERSTANDING

Understanding begins with highly developed awareness. You need to make a conscious effort to continuously improve your own level of awareness and understanding if you desire to master communications.

Most people are primarily focused on themselves. However, this does not mean they are fully aware of who they are, why they behave the way they do, or precisely what their intentions are. The harsh reality is they have a very limited view of the world and other people. They are ignorant. This statement is not an indictment or accusation of inferior intelligence, and it is very different from being dumb or stupid. Some people just don't know f they don't know. They are unconscious of their incompetence.

This is especially true of self-awareness. As Joseph LeDoux noted in his book *Synaptic Self*, brain research has discovered that "the way we characteristically walk and talk and even the way we think and feel all reflect the workings of systems that function on the basis of past experience, but their operation takes place outside of awareness."[1]

Science is making gigantic leaps in the study of communications, people's behavior, and, more specifically, the human brain. Many ideas that have been passed from generation to generation as old wives' tales are now being validated and backed up by scientific research. Other ideas that have been assumed as true are being altered or debunked. In

Synaptic Self, LeDoux discusses the evolution of scientific thought about the brain. In 1770, Anton Mesmer, a Viennese physician, found he could affect patients by looking into their eyes and waving his hands over the afflicted body part. This was the birth of hypnosis. In 1895 Sigmund Freud theorized that the nervous system consists of distinct and similarly constructed neurons. In 1950, the electron microscope allowed scientists to actually see the tiny spaces, synaptic spaces, between fibers extending out of neurons. So what were these early pioneers actually doing, and how does the brain work? At the risk of being overly simplistic, let's look at a few relevant scientific findings.

One of the fundamental insights is that signals are sent between neurons without actual contact, but rather across open space, the synaptic spaces, and it is done by alternating electrical and chemical events. Mesmer started helping people by using magnets and soon learned that he could influence his patients without using magnets or physical contact, the beginning of hypnosis.

Freud was on to something very big, a neural theory of memory and consciousness, but chose to leave his scientific research and plunged into a purely psychological explanation for his findings. We now know that chemicals and electricity are critical parts of brain function. We also know that the brain can be changed by new experiences and repetition of events.

Therefore, think of the impact of diet and exercise on the way your brain functions. Many behaviors we practice in our daily routines are in reality a form of self-medication. Coffee, soda, MSG, chocolate, running, strength training, and sex all cause a chemical reaction in our brain. Starbucks loves the addictive impact of caffeine on their customers, and Nike advocates to "just do it" and enjoy the runner's high, obviously in your Nike running shoes. What do you think are the intentions of these companies? Are you conscious and aware of why you behave the way you do? Who's in control?

Nature Versus Nurture

The debate of nature versus nurture is alive and well. Both have a significant place in understanding why we behave the way we do and how the brain works. Our genetic makeup is very important as it relates to behavior, personality, and longevity. The problem is we don't choose our parents, so we have no choice in the genes we inherit.

The really exciting news is that our brain has plasticity, the ability to change as a result of experience. This means that how we behave and who we are can change. The most dramatic changes comes in the first few years of our life or as a result of trauma. However, science has discovered that our brain is constantly changing and can be influenced to change up until death. The computer slogan "garbage in, garbage out" is true for our body and our brain. The same is true for muscle development. Studies have shown that even the elderly can build muscle and increase bone strength with regular exercise. Exercise will improve your mood and help avoid depression. Your muscles and your brain improve and grow with more use.

The more knowledge you have about how and why people behave the way they do, the better you will be able to control and influence yourself and others. This chapter focuses on numerous areas in order to expand your perspective. These areas are critical for you to understand and learn to use. Don't forget that success is a journey and not a destination. Your discovery, learning, and practice will continue for years to come.

A little knowledge can be a dangerous thing. When you make decisions and come to conclusions based on insufficient information, you may actually create more problems. Your knowledge must be comprehensive and applied to be useful. When you consistently combine knowledge and continual learning with experience, you will make great progress. To significantly change your life and create a masterpiece requires a decision, commitment, and persistent effort. Significant and lasting change does not happen by simply reading a good book or attending a great seminar. This may start the process, but it takes time and consistency to really change.

Your life is dynamic, and there is always more to learn; new discoveries are being made regularly. Your task is to stay current, continually be a student, and realize that things are always changing. A good example of this principle in contemporary society is technology. In 1965, Gordon E. Moore, co-founder of Intel, wrote a paper discussing how fast the components in integrated circuits were doubling. Building on this idea in 1970, a Caltech professor coined the phrase "Moore's Law" to describe the concept of continuous growth and perpetual doubling. If you prefer a historical perspective, consider that many centuries ago, even before Plato, Heraclitus said, "The only thing that is constant is change."[2]

Your Assignment

So, how can you begin using *The CEO Code* as a catalyst to significant, positive, and lasting change? A simple visualization of this chapter and this book is to think of being in a building with no windows. Not only would you be in a dark place, it would be very difficult to know what is going on outside and hard to judge the changes in the external environment. Let's imagine that you decide to punch a hole in the wall and begin a process of installing windows.

If the building had just one window you would have a limited view and perspective. Obviously, if you added more windows you would increase your awareness and understanding of where you were and what the external environment was like. The key is to remember that each window gives you a bit more insight. Each window is accurate based on its orientation, and sometimes the view from one window is different from the view from another window. No single window is able to give you a complete 360 degree view of your total environment or situation, so the more windows the better.

Have you ever been in a public place, maybe a restaurant or local gathering place, and someone comes in who changes the whole atmosphere of the place because he is loud and brash with his comments to people he knows and doesn't know? Did you want to go up to him and tell him to cool it? Did you think about just leaving because he was were so rude?

Years ago I found myself in this situation at my favorite local restaurant. A business executive in a pinstriped suit and tie arrived and made a grand entrance. He was loud, laughed boisterously, and let the entire restaurant know he was there. Customers in the restaurant were noticeably uncomfortable and annoyed. I chose to ignore him.

Well, as the years passed, I had occasion to see him a few more times. He was always the same: loud, rude, and trying to be the center of attention. Then about two years ago, I was sitting at the bar waiting for my dinner table, and this same rude and obnoxious guy came in and sat down next to me. It was decision time. Do I move, ignore him, or wait for the right opening and tell him where to go? Well, I chose to do none of the above. I waited for the right moment and then very gently looked him straight in the eye, greeted him, and introduced myself in a soft and reserved voice. "Hi. How are you? My name is David Rohlander."

It was obvious to me that, as he did a double-take, he wasn't sure how to react. After a second he yelled back his name and boldly said, "I'm great." I responded calmly and gradually was able to mellow out our discourse and start a conversation. We talked for well more than a half hour.

I discovered that he's actually a good guy who has had some real challenges in life. This particular night he was upset because he had just had a school conference about his son, who was in junior high school. The boy had a few learning disabilities and was not performing at an acceptable level for the teacher. Dad was upset.

You guessed it—nature versus nurture. The father has the same learning disabilities; both father and son have a severe hearing impairment. During our conversation, he shared how he has had to cope with these issues and how often, when he was young, people would push him around and take advantage of him because he wasn't able to hear well and he didn't learn as fast as some of the other kids. As a young man, he learned to cope by being aggressive and loud. As he said in our conversation, "The best defense is a strong offense."

As this example shows, there are reasons behind someone's conduct. The more a person understands how to recognize these differences and nuances of behavior in people, the better she will be able to relate to and deal with the multitude of variations in people. Learning to understand people is very similar to peeling an onion; both people and onions have many layers. *The CEO Code* is not an attempt to make you a psychologist, psychiatrist, scientist, or a doctor. Rather, think of yourself as a mechanic. Focus on the immediate situation and what is going on, and then decide what you need to know and do to get the car to run so you can go from point A to point B.

Let's get started exploring the various areas critical to understanding people. Think of each of these areas as one of the windows in the dark building mentioned earlier. The more, better, and bigger your knowledge base and understanding is, the easier it is to see out of the building, your situation, and effectively communicate with others.

Body Language

One of the most obvious and helpful windows that you want to install in your building of knowledge is a comprehensive understanding of body language. It is impossible to not communicate through body language. A person's body language is always saying something. Take a look at someone's posture: Is he moving and energetic, stiff, or totally relaxed? Take note of hand gestures, personal space given or taken away, and the focus of attention or lack of attention. When he talks or listens, how engaged is he with the other person? Is he closed and egocentric, or open and inclusive?

You want to always look at the whole picture. Body language is most insightful when you observe the entire person, not just one gesture or position. You also want to take into consideration the patterns of movement, expression, and posture. Realize that a person may have her arms crossed because she is cold, not because she is closed off to you.

Notice the speed of movement, the size of movement, and the refinement of movement. How does this compare to the way the person talks? Is she bold and loud, or soft and reserved? Is her posture rigid or relaxed? Are her voice, tone, facial expression, and words congruent? What does she do with her hands and feet? Is she open and bold with the position of her hands and feet? Does she keep her hands close to her body or touch her face?

Most importantly, look at his face. What is the expression? Does he have a ready and easy smile, or is he stone-faced? Notice the combination of the person's facial expression and eyes. The eyes are the most effective body language tool anyone has. By becoming a student of the eyes, you can learn to read a person like a book. There is an entire discipline called personology, which studies the relationship between physical structure, especially the face, of humans and their behavior.

Learning to use and interpret body language is an art form, like dancing. There are many very specific steps or movements, but it is experiencing the whole that is the most insightful. It is not something for which you learn one movement or position and then mechanically do it; it is continual movement, gesture, and expression. To become aware of the many elements of body language and the way people communicate, observe, observe, and observe some more.

Studying people closely reminds me of carefully observing your surroundings while walking in the woods. If you normally live and work in the city and have occasion to go to the country, you will have to adjust to this new environment. Let's assume you are taking your first walk in the woods; you are probably more concerned about where you are going and how to get there than what's going on around you. Think about stopping, standing still, and looking and listening to what's going on around you. Do you hear the birds? Is there wind in the trees? Can you see which side of the tree the moss is on?

Are you aware of the subtle signals and environmental warnings in the forest? The birds often give notice of a stranger in the woods and sound a warning to other birds. The air moves more in the tops of the trees than at ground level. You might see movement in the branches of the trees more than feel it in your face.

Where is the wind coming from? One way to identify the wind direction is to moisten your finger in your mouth and then hold it up to the air. The cool side is where the breeze is coming from. If you are in the northern hemisphere, the sun shines the least on the north side of the trees; therefore moss has a tendency to grow on the north side of tree trunks. That is a simple way to orient yourself if you can't see the sun because of tree cover or overcast weather.

These clues in nature are just like the clues we get from people when we are trying to communicate with them. Reading people's body language is equally simple if you develop focus and awareness. Start with observing the eyes and facial expression. Do they look at you and smile, or do they just pass by looking straight ahead? A glance and twinkle in the eye are signs of openness. A glance and no change in expression or turning away show lack of interest in you. This may be because of anxiety, fear, displeasure, or simply having something pressing on their agenda or mind.

When in a discussion with others, notice how and when they move. A sign of interest is when they lean into the discussion. A shift in body position often is a sign of increased interest or possibly that the discussion has become uncomfortable.

How can you tell if someone is telling the truth? There are some simple signals to look for, but be sure you don't leap to conclusions because of one gesture. When a person tells a lie, he may unconsciously do any combination of the following: change the tone of his voice, shift his eyes away, pass his hand in front of his mouth or over the ear, or break or pause his speech, possibly even giving a quick, defensive response.

Behavioral Styles

Our first window helped us see and understand body language. Let's create another hole in the building and install another window of knowledge: behavioral styles. Have you ever asked yourself, "Why isn't everyone normal like me?" Well, if you have, you are not alone. Most people try to figure out why others behave the way they do, and how to predict and handle those weird and strange ones that are so very different than "me."

One of the first people to record and analyze the different types of behavior in people was Hippocrates. He thought it had something to do with the type of body a person had. Some people believe it's all in the structure of a person's face. Others rely on the place and time of birth, and still others feel environment has a lot to do with behavior. Well, I believe all of these things have some truth.

I'd like to share with you an elementary paradigm that has served me well for more than 20 years and that will give you more insight than any other single approach. It will be your most revealing window in your effort to build more knowledge and understanding. When you choose to ignore the differences in people and treat everyone the same way, you are only successful or effective a small percentage of the time. The way you or anybody behaves with other people is very complex, because many factors determine behavior. These factors include your past experiences, cultural background, environment, temperament, and even your age. Yet, everyone has developed behavioral patterns, or distinct ways of thinking, feeling, and acting. If you learn to recognize these patterns, you will improve your ability to communicate with the infinite variety of people you encounter every day. You don't have to become a psychologist or a psychiatrist. Just remember what the late, great comedian Flip Wilson would say when he was dressed up like "Geraldine": "What you see is what you get."

Everyone is unique. Your task is to be able to recognize the differences and respond accordingly. A good way to look at it is to imagine that different people speak different languages. When you understand other people rapidly and are able to speak their language, you will be able to help them get what they want and need. If you are only able to effectively communicate with people "just like you" (who speak *your* language) then you will be successful a small percentage of the time.

So let's go to language school. The first thing to remember is that even though this is straightforward and relatively simple, it takes time and practice to make this a part of you. Many people "know about" the Seven Habits, TQM, Open Book Management, ISO 9001, and Re-Engineering. But the real question should be: How many people have internalized the concepts? Many know about them, several can talk about them, a few use some of the principles, but it is rare to find someone who has mastered the particular paradigm.

There are basically four styles of behavior or, in our analogy, languages. No single style stands purely on its own. We all use a combination of these styles and often switch to different styles depending on our environment.

Direct (D)

These people stand out in the crowd. A really strong Direct (D) has a horrible time waiting in line. She is impatient. Not only is she impatient, but she has a tendency to tell others what to do. It never enters her mind to gently ask for something, because she believes it is important to get things done: "I want action and I want it now!" You might notice she seems to have a big ego. That often is obvious when she interrupts others, gives orders, or seems to just roll over other people.

Influencer (I)

My, how these people are charming! The Influencer (I) is usually very talkative. This is his most obvious giveaway. He talks a lot and is very emotional, animated, and enthusiastic. Persuasion comes naturally to the Influencer. When a job requires quiet focus without other people involved, it can be difficult for an Influencer to stay on task. He loves to discuss issues and tends to be personally involved with the people around him.

Steady (S)

Studies show that the majority of people are primarily this style. Remember: We are all a combination of all four, but Steady is most common as the dominant part of most people's style. I like to call these people the salt of the earth. A steady is dependable, agreeable, and calm. Her tendency is to enjoy a strong group or family orientation, and be a bit on the reserved side. She resists change, and seeks stability and security. "Can't we just get along?" could be her motto.

Cautious (C)

>These people are often perfectionists. "Everything in its place and a place for everything" would be the guiding principle for a Cautious (C). They find it easy to stay focused on a task, because they don't need the amount of personal interaction typical of an Influencer. A Cautious person prefers less small talk and is very sensitive, especially to criticism. However, he is often preoccupied with finding faults in others. Because he strives for precision and order, it is difficult to find a mistake he's made. Don't try to do this, or at least don't mention it. It's akin to trying to find a flea on a porcupine.

When a Direct or Cautious find things are not going the way they want them to go, they may appear abrasive. The Direct will become more assertive and the Cautious will become more critical. The Influencer and the Steady will tend to be more amiable if they are not getting what they want. The Influencer will try to persuade people to get his way while the Steady will be patient and flexible.

The better you learn to speak another person's language, the friendlier they become. I lived in Europe for three years. At first, I struggled with the language and found people were not particularly friendly. I enrolled in German classes, studied, practiced, and embarrassed myself many times. Ultimately, I became conversant in German. My relationships with the German people changed; they became more and more friendly. I believe it was because they realized I had taken the time to understand them and their language. I firmly believe the more you understand another person, her goals, and her fears, and learn to speak her language, the better you will be able to communicate. Effective communication requires more than talent. It involves trust, respect, *understanding*, empathy, and resolution.

Everyone has certain ways they behave in relation to other people. Throughout our lives, we each become comfortable with a certain way of acting that reflects our thinking and our feelings. Sometimes we are required to adjust our normal, instinctive way of behaving to adapt to a new or unusual situation. These are learned responses. The specific and unique combination of our learned and instinctive responses is our individual style.

It pays to look for patterns when you communicate with others, because all people exhibit the four distinctive styles of behavior. Each person has a unique combination of these four behavioral styles and usually favors one above the others. When you are able to identify another person's preferred style, you will be able to dramatically improve your ability to communicate with that person.

Again, it is virtually impossible for a person not to communicate. The simple fact of not talking, having minimal facial expression, and being reserved provides a lot of information to others about who you are, what your goals are, and what you fear. By mastering personal styles, you will be able to make these assessments quickly and with a high level of accuracy.

The first thing you want to take note of when interacting with others is whether they have a tendency to be expressive or reserved. Are they extroverts or introverts? The extroverts will be either "Ds" or "Is," for which D stands for Direct or Dominant and I stands for Influencing or Interest in people. By the same token, when you identify a person with reserved or shy behaviors, you are probably dealing with either an "S," meaning Steadiness or Stability, or a "C," someone who is Compliant or Cautious.

You may quickly and accurately identify your own behavioral style by taking a short assessment on my Website: *www.DavidRohlander. com/assessments/*. When you are able to tell if the other person is outgoing or more laid back, you have narrowed his primary style from one of four to one of two. You now have a 50-50 chance of knowing what his style is.

The high D will be more intense, be straightforward, and tell people what to do. The high I will probably be very expressive with his or her face, show lots of emotion, and talk a lot. It's not as easy with the S and C people. The high S is laid back, group-oriented, and amiable, whereas the high C is more formal, reserved, and very precise, as well as rule-oriented.

It's amusing to think of famous politicians and what behavioral styles they exhibit. The classic D might be a Ross Perot; he was too much of a D to get elected. If you search for a high I in the dictionary, you will find a picture of Bill Clinton. The S is best exemplified by the first Bush, George H.W. Bush. And an example of a high C is Jimmy Carter.

Let's look at the goal of each style.

Style	Goal
D Direct/Dominant	To be in control
I Influencing/Interest in people	To be socially approved
S Steadiness/Stability	To have security/ stability
C Compliance/ Competence	To have everything in order

Do you see how these goals are correlated to the way each of the politicians mentioned behave? Ross Perot was always trying to tell the journalist how to do the interview, and then he would pull out his charts and become a pedantic teacher. Bill Clinton loves the adoration of people; he needs lots of people around him. On his last day in the White House, he went to the airport after all the ceremonies, gave another goodbye speech, and said he would be around for a long time and for his followers to stay close. George H.W. Bush was very good at building relationships with leaders from other nations; that's why he had the security of many alliance partners going into the first war in Iraq. He also knew all his Secret Service details personally. Jimmy Carter was big on people doing it his way and in order. He boycotted the Olympics in 1980, because Russia invaded Afghanistan, and is well-known for criticizing current presidents, whether they are Republican or Democrat.

The chart on page 64 shows an outline of each of the styles with their primary characteristics, goals, and fears. This is a model that is easy to master and will give you invaluable insight into why and how people are behaving. I encourage you to study this model, practice it, and share it with coworkers, family, and customers. It is worth the time to learn and make a part of your conscious and unconscious thinking. This means more than just knowing about it; extend the effort to internalize it. If you need help, e-mail me at David@DavidRohlander.com or phone me directly at (714) 771–7043. It's that important!

Most people favor a combination of two or sometimes just one of the styles. However, we all have some of each of the four behavioral styles. The behavioral style of a person is usually different in each unique situation. For example, when you are in a familiar situation, you may behave like an "I," and when you are in a strange or new situation, you may become more reserved and critical, behaving more like a "C."

"D" Dominant	"I" Influential
Direct	Talkative
Impatient	Outgoing
Action-oriented	People-oriented
Bottom line/results-focused	Enthusiastic
Uses telling behaviors	Persuasive

GOAL
  Results and Control
	GOAL
	  Recognition and approval

FEAR
  Losing control
  Being taken advantage of
	FEAR
	  Rejection
	  Social disapproval

"S" Steady	"C" Competence
Supportive	Cautious
Easygoing	Cool and distant
Process-oriented	Facts-oriented
Likes people, relaxed	Evaluates pros and cons
Unemotional, low key	Self-disciplined

GOAL
  Stability and security
	GOAL
	  Precision and order

FEAR
  Sudden change
  Losing security
	FEAR
	  Violation of standards
	  Criticism of performance

Being able to read a person's behavioral style gives you many advantages when trying to effectively communicate with another person. A person's style will impact his use of time as well as the manner in which he chooses to interact with people. When planning your day, take into consideration the different styles of the people at work and in your personal life. An "I" will enjoy talking. A "D" will often be in a hurry. The "S" and "C" like thorough explanations.

Once you have studied and learned how to read others, it's time to adjust your behavior to "speak" the other person's language. Remember: This does not mean that you change your own personal values or compromise what you believe. You are merely adjusting your language.

Intelligence

There are many types of intelligence. In our analogy, this is like having an entire wall of huge windows to let in light. When I was in elementary school, there was a focus on reading, writing, and arithmetic. These areas were most important if you wanted to go to college. At my high school, they had wood shop, home economics, and typing for kids who didn't want to go to college. We have come a long way since those years of limited choices and views.

Howard Gardner, professor of cognition and education at the Harvard Graduate School of Education, has developed a Theory of Multiple Intelligences. According to this theory, there are several types of intelligence that work independently and together to solve problems for the brain. This is consistent with the concept of multiple brain systems proposed by Joseph LeDoux. LeDoux describes the brain as having several computers working in parallel, each used separately and also in concert to operate the body, think, remember, and solve problems. Each system has a given amount of capability, and they are not all equal. This has more to do with nature than with nurture. Gardner suggests that we all have different amounts of intelligence in the various defined areas, and while we are growing up there is an ebb and flow of development in each of these areas.

This is important to you as a leader because everyone has a unique amount of each type of intelligence. They will be most productive when they are focused on work that requires utilizing their given type of intelligence. All people need to focus on their strengths to achieve at high levels. So let's briefly review the types of intelligences that Gardner has identified in his research.

1. **Linguistic/Verbal**—likes to read and write; good at memorizing data.

2. **Mathematical/Logical**—likes numbers and asking questions; good at math and logic.

3. **Spatial**—likes to draw, build, and design; good at imagining, puzzles, and maps.

4. **Musical**—likes to sing, hum, and play music; good at deciphering music and rhythm.

5. **Body/Kinesthetic**—likes movement and touch; good at sports, dance, and crafts.

6. **Interpersonal**—likes people, talking, and groups; good at reading people and influencing others.

7. **Intrapersonal**—likes to work alone; good at self-management, instincts, and goals.

When I was being tested to qualify for pilot training, there were rigorous physical standards, as well as reading, writing, and arithmetic tests. The U.S. Air Force also tested me for spatial intelligence; it was my highest score. To fly fighters, you have to be able to relate the map to the ground, as well as creatively grasp spatial relationships and maneuver the plane upside down, twisting and turning while making split-second decisions. Spatial intelligence is critical.

When my son was in junior high school, he was given a battery of assessments. It turns out he is gifted. However, his highest score was in spatial intelligence. This was a significant finding and has helped him in his chosen career as an artist.

One other window of understanding that we need to look through is emotional intelligence, or EI. Much of the brain research that we have briefly reviewed here has been combined over the last few decades by scientists and medical researchers using newer technologies and studies. It is difficult to say who first identified and coined the phrase *emotional intelligence*. It is an extension of the work done by Howard Gardner, specifically in the areas of interpersonal and intrapersonal intelligence mentioned previously.

EI is important to you because it has been demonstrated over and over that emotional intelligence is critical to success and achievement within organizations and businesses. Many believe it is the trump card over all other forms of intelligence. The reason for this is because good decisions and effectively dealing with people cannot be done without EI. Two easy-to-read books that give a thorough explanation are *Emotional Intelligence* and *Primal Leadership*, both by Daniel Goleman.

The five basic elements of emotional intelligence are:

1. **Being aware of yourself.** This has everything to do with being aware of your own personal feelings, being able to observe the way you are behaving in a given situation, and understanding how the behavior is connected to your emotions.

2. **Managing your own emotions.** It's one thing to know how you feel, it is a totally different thing to be able to manage those feelings. Think about when you experience fear, anger, guilt, power, lust, or security; are you able to control and manage each of these emotions?

3. **Motivating yourself.** Some rely on outside stimuli to get motivated. Do you use your internal self to create and do those things that you don't feel like doing?

4. **Being able to identify the emotions of others.** Do you read people well? Do you appreciate with empathy the way they feel, as well as understand some of the emotional issues they may have that are inhibiting their performance?

5. **Influencing personal relationships.** Dr. Paul Hersey says that leadership is influence. How effectively do you influence others on an emotional level? Do you inspire them? Do you create confidence and caring for others so that they want to follow your lead?

These concepts come easier to some than to others. However, all of us can improve the way we understand and practice our interpersonal relationships, and develop more facility with the emotional side of those relationships. First comes understanding, then we start to experiment and practice. (The Execution section of this book gives you a practical game plan on how to improve in this area.)

Emotions play a big role in what you remember. It can be said that memory is emotion-specific. When you try to recall events from your youth, you will probably realize that you remember things that have had a significant emotional component to them. Where there are intense emotional experiences, there is enduring memory. What this means to you is that when you factor in past experience as a partial explanation of why people behave the way they do, it is obvious that strong emotional reactions have more to do with a person's past than anything else. For example, the whole topic of what is acceptable for a person is mostly based on that person's own personal past experiences. From a practical point of view, that is why it is so important for you to get to know your employees well. Each person has had different past experiences, and those experiences have a huge impact on his emotional state, values, and point of view.

The real nuance is that most people do not realize that the reason they act or react the way they do is because of their past experiences. Ever hear someone say "I don't know why I feel that way. I just do"? Often, the brain's "fight or flight" trigger, the amygdala, is activated by unconscious memories, rather than conscious ones.

One of my coaching clients, a vice president of a Fortune 500 company, was incredibly competent at the technical aspects of his job, but was having issues with his staff because he would lose his temper, yell, and say damaging things. The CEO was most concerned because, in our litigious society, the VP's behavior was potentially exposing the company to a lawsuit. His future with the company was in jeopardy.

This ultimately became a great coaching opportunity. The VP client understood the potential liability and desperately wanted to keep his very lucrative job. We covered many topics during our coaching sessions, but the real issue was helping him develop emotional intelligence. It worked. He has since received a promotion and is doing well.

Artful Congruence

As I've stated previously, effective communication requires more than talent. It involves trust, respect, understanding, empathy, and resolution. It is an art. This is the approach developed through the years that has worked very well for me and my clients. Talent will take you just so far and no further. To truly achieve, to create art, you must go beyond talent. Have you ever thought of making your communication an art form? Do people thank you for the way you dialogue with them? When you encounter people, do you create a unique communication experience for them?

I have learned a lot from my son, an accomplished artist. Nathan won his first art contest in first grade, and has since won many awards and created a successful career as a painter. He graduated from Art Center College of Design with honors several years ago, and was recently invited to come back as an instructor. Being recognized in this way by one of the finest art schools in the world is a tribute to his talent and, more importantly, his years of hard work.

Let's review a few principles from art that relate directly to you becoming a great leader. First, Nathan spends more time thinking about what he will paint than actually painting. We call that planning. Once he knows what he wants to create, the execution goes quickly.

Second, the reason it goes quickly is because his skill level is extremely high. He has invested hours, days, and years in practicing the basics. He is always sketching. He once joined me at a seminar and sketched the speaker. In restaurants, I have often seen him sketch people at another table. If you check out his Website, *www.Rohlander.com*, you'll see sketches from when he had a part-time job at the House of Blues on Sunset Boulevard while working on his MFA.

Third, having your own unique style, or what might be called a personal brand, takes time to develop. Nathan has studied great artists in books, museums, and galleries all over the world, even experimenting by copying their brush strokes and drawing the way they did. Through time, he has grown and developed his own way.

You may have great talent, but you must apply it and work hard. Michael Jordan has great talent in basketball, and he attained seven scoring titles and three championships; he worked hard. Edwin Moses has great talent at running the hurdles and won 107 consecutive finals; he worked hard. They say Michael Phelps's body is designed to swim, plus he has talent and is the most decorated Olympian of all time, but most importantly, he worked hard. No matter what your chosen field is—art, sports, or business—it is going to take hard work.

Congruence comes about by knowing your own beliefs, being able to articulate those beliefs, and manifesting those same beliefs by your behavior. Essentially, you are able to walk the talk. People are watching you all the time, and when you are in harmony, they see your beliefs, goals, and priorities by watching your behavior. You become artfully congruent when you master the knowing and the doing so well that you are unconsciously competent and totally consistent.

Congratulations to you for reading this book. To create a masterpiece personally and professionally, you need to totally master the basics, practice, and work hard. *The CEO Code* is a practical guide to mastering the attitudes, knowledge, skills, and behaviors required to master leadership and build a great company. This chapter covered key topics in the knowledge area that are requisite to becoming a more effective communicator. You now can focus on each of them one at a time. Study and experiment with them as you continue to grow and learn.

We have used a metaphor of creating windows to expand you understanding. The three primary areas we discussed are body language, behavioral styles, and multiple intelligences. In addition to these core areas you may also want to study neurolinguistic programming (NLP), speaking skills, and, most importantly, listening skills. These areas will all help you understand communication better. For more information on resources, seminars, and workshops go to *www.DavidRohlander.com*.

Take Time to Reflect

As you contemplate this chapter, take a few minutes alone and answer these questions.

1. What do other people do that annoys you?

2. Are you able to trace your background and discover why you feel annoyed by others?

3. How often do you ask for and get feedback from others about your behavior?

4. Can you identify behaviors in your personal life and professional life that need to improve? Do you have a written plan to implement the improvement?

5. When analyzing your own body language, how much do you consciously control?

6. Which types of multiple intelligences are your strongest? Which are your weakest?

7. What did you learn about yourself by taking the personal behavioral assessment on *www.DavidRohlander.com*?

Chapter 4

Empathy

*Constant kindness can accomplish much. As the sun
makes ice melt, kindness causes misunderstanding,
mistrust, and hostility to evaporate.*

—Albert Schweitzer

Several years ago, I was invited to a fundraiser by a friend and business associate. He was calling in a favor, and this event was for a good cause. It was called the ADD Holiday Celebration. December is a busy month, with time spent getting ready for family vacations, buying gifts, and trying to wind up the year with that final push to maximize sales and profits. Nevertheless, I wrote the check and decided to go to this event anyway.

ADD stands for Advocates for the Developmentally Disabled. The purpose of the event was to raise money and awareness among churches, synagogues, and other religious organizations in order to include people with disabilities in meetings, services, and classes. Attitudes are a lot different now, but back then people had a tendency to ignore or avoid those in our society who were severely different.

When the night of the event arrived, we took special care to wear not only fine threads, but also to honor the spirit of the season and wear bright colors. I wore the classic pinstriped suit and a red tie. My wife always looks good and dresses elegantly, though, if the truth be told, I don't remember exactly what she wore that night!

Let me share with you what I do remember. We arrived at the hotel and, on the way to the ballroom, greeted many friends we knew from the local business community. I was surprised to hear a band playing as we entered the room. As we approached our table, I was pleased to see an attorney friend and his wife sitting at our table. I didn't know the other six people, so I decided it was a chance to make new friends.

A minister welcomed everyone during his opening remarks, and then a rabbi offered a prayer. During the meal, we enjoyed pleasant conversation, while in the background the band played songs that had a holiday theme. I happened to notice that the band was small and that some of the band members looked uncomfortable in formal black attire.

It turns out that the band was composed of students from Hope School in Anaheim, and they all had various types of disabilities. For example, there was a blind piano player. Despite their disabilities, several of the students were brilliant musicians, and I was pleased to hear really good music.

Part of the program was to sing holiday songs. A tall, slender student led the singing in his rich baritone voice. When the band started playing "Jingle Bells," the song leader left the podium, microphone in hand, and started walking among the large round tables of guests.

As he approached our table, he noticed I was singing along. Suddenly I realized he was coming directly at me. He reached out for my hand, helped me stand up, and then put the microphone in my face. Because I am an experienced singer and didn't want to look like a wimp, I continued to sing and made sure to add a bit more energy and volume. At the end of the song, everyone clapped.

Embarrassed, I tried to sit down but I wasn't fast enough. The tall song leader reached out, put his hands on my shoulders, and proceeded to give me a big hug. Now, I am 6'2" and he was 4 to 5 inches taller than me. He then held me at arm's length, and while looking me straight in the eye, said, "I love you."

As we stood there, looking at each other, in front of nearly 300 people, I experienced a warmth and sincerity that was absolutely remarkable. I remember it to this day. It reminds me of a quote from Dr. Maya Angelou, the famous American poet: "I've learned that people will forget what you said, people will forget what you did, but people will never forget how you made them feel."[1]

You and I need to remind ourselves that other people will remember how we make them feel. I doubt many of the 300 people at that banquet remember our duet, but I do. What surprises me is how often it is the little things that create lasting memories for us.

Let me share a few examples. Do you remember the time you went out of your way to hold the door open for another person? Some people think they are so important that they don't ever hold the door for another person. If you've ever done this, did you ever wonder what the person who got blocked or beat to the door was feeling? How about the person who is so self-absorbed that she doesn't even have the inclination to greet people, much less to share a smile? Many people are on a mission and just charge through the office to do *important things*, totally ignoring their coworkers.

My "favorite" is the person who is engaged in a conversation with you and his cell phone rings. Without hesitation, he picks it up, pushes the phone on, and turns away while launching into a new phone conversation. No "excuse me," "I'm sorry, I have to get this," or any sign of recognition that he was engaged in a conversation with you. How does that make *you* feel?

These behaviors are evidence of a person's low level of emotional intelligence, EI. The beginning of EI is being aware of yourself, then being aware of others. As we develop new knowledge, attitudes, and skills in the emotional arena, it influences our behavior. We will change our feelings and we will change the feelings we impart to others.

You are in control of your own feelings, and when you have developed EI, you are able to significantly influence the feelings of others. Effective communication requires both parties to be empathetic. Throughout this book, I will be sharing specific tools and methods to help you enhance your knowledge and skills so you will be able to master communication, execution, and operations. If you communicate really well with people, it is all about *you*. By the same token, if you have difficulty communicating with others, it is also all about *you*. You are your own solution.

Choice

At a very fundamental level, all attitudes and behaviors can be identified as initially coming from either fear or love. This bifurcated view has roots in spiritual philosophies from both the Eastern and Western traditions. It is also embraced by most psychologists. Our interest, however, is results-focused and based on practical business experience. What are the benefits that can be derived by understanding this simple perspective?

When you are insecure, judgmental, or worried about control and yourself, there is a tendency to attack, withdraw, or become a victim. These behaviors are probably coming from fear. Have you ever seen a boss yell at another person? How about the manager who just walks out of the room in disgust, mumbling under her breath? I know you have heard a leader opine that the lack of positive results and achievement is "not my fault." All of these negative behaviors have an origin based in fear and low self-concept.

There are four specific behaviors that are severe warning signs of impending failure in a relationship. They are criticism, contempt, defensiveness, and withdrawal. This concept, known as "The Four Horsemen," is from research by Dr. John M. Gottman and is based on intensive, detailed, and long-term scientific study of why marriages succeed or fail.

There is an alternative to this type of negative behavior. You do not need to come from a place of fear and low self-concept. The choice is yours. Take some time for self-examination, and think about why and how you might want to work on your own self-concept and behaviors.

So what is a better solution? Obviously, it is preferable to come from a position of love, caring, and positive energy. Implicit in this view are personal responsibility, self-confidence, and awareness of your own feelings, as well as the feelings of others. This perspective does not come easily for many people. It may require training, coaching, and even study. It is a process that requires you to be so confident and comfortable with yourself that you are ready, willing, and able to completely focus on the other person. Your agenda will then be to understand and help discover positive solutions or outcomes.

A helpful way to comprehend this concept is illustrated by thinking back to when you were learning to read and write in school. Remember when you had to conjugate a verb? Specifically, let's look at the verb "to be." First person singular is "I am," second person singular is "you are," and third person singular is "he, she, it is." What grade were you in when you first learned this? For me it was in grammar school with Mrs. Duffy, the same teacher who made me write on the blackboard "Is is a linking verb" two hundred times!

When you are communicating, listening, or expressing empathy, remember to be mostly in the second person—the "you are." It is also helpful in sales, advertising, and personal relationships to primarily be in the second person. Next time you hear a speech, especially by a politician, pay attention to how many times the speaker uses the pronoun

"I" versus the pronoun "you." If you are typical of most people, you will appreciate when they talk to *you* and probably feel they are egocentric and narcissistic if they use a lot of "I." It reminds me of that old adage attributed to Theodore Roosevelt: "Nobody cares how much you know, until they know how much you care."[2]

As discussed in the previous chapter on understanding, each of us has a unique personal past experience that has, in large measure, influenced the way we behave now. Take time to reflect on why you act the way you do, and think about the benefits of making some gradual or maybe dramatic changes in your behavior. This will then lead you to a natural period of growth, when you are able to clearly focus on what your intentions are and bring your behaviors into sync with your intentions.

When your intention is to lead with love rather than fear, you will notice some very distinct behavioral patterns. You will be open to being influenced by others. You will be willing to experience some temporary pain, fear, or hurt in order to learn the truth about yourself or the real situation within the company. You will take the time and interest to understand why certain people feel the way they do about you or the situation. This is all possible because you are secure in who you are. Your self-confidence is a product of your own understanding. It is not dependent on others praising or giving you their approval. You are results focused. As a leader, you rejoice and celebrate your people, and reward them for finding solutions.

Other People

It is not easy to manage people effectively. In business, there are many decisions that must be made. Some think the way to make decisions should be based on purely logical, analytical, and practical considerations. More than one of my clients has expressed the desire and preference to work with machines, computers, or even alone. These clients have difficulty understanding what makes people tick.

When I started in business many years ago, managers were practical and pragmatic. They focused on business, not people. There was little or no regard for emotional concerns. You came in on time or early, did your job, often worked overtime, and went home. It was not appropriate to discuss your personal life or express emotion too much. "Rohlander, you are here to produce" was a phrase I often heard. One of my managers at Merrill Lynch had a wood carving on the center of his desk facing out so it was impossible to not read it as you stood in front of him; it was clearly visible and totally consistent with his intentions. It said "Produce or Perish."

Results are important. However, the fact is that when you have an employee who cares, leads a balanced life, and takes personal responsibility for more than just producing money, you get better and bigger results. An executive who only focuses on making money is a very shallow person. A similar sentiment was expressed by Henry Ford in 1903, when he said, "A business that makes nothing but money is a poor business."[3]

Any experienced salesperson knows that the buying decision is triggered by emotion and then justified by facts and figures. Empathy is all about being able to relate to another person on an emotional level, understanding how and why they feel the way they do.

Your expression of empathy is the emotional trigger that enables another person to believe you actually care. Now, if in addition to this expression of sincere empathy, you add behaviors that demonstrate clearly that people can trust you, and you treat them with respect, you will be well on the way to effectively communicating. Can you see why, if you remove or compromise any one of these three (trust, respect, or empathy), you will have difficulty developing quality communications?

All of this is meant to deepen your understanding of how to effectively communicate. The final step is to come to resolution. That's our next chapter.

Take Time to Reflect

As you contemplate this chapter, take a few minutes alone and answer these questions.

1. What little things do you do to be nice to people?

2. How well do you read appreciation from others if they don't say anything?

3. What do you say or do to show how much you care?

4. Do your behaviors and actions come from a fear- or love-oriented core belief system?

5. When you listen to another person is it to understand or to judge?

6. Are you able to consciously focus on communicating in the second person?

7. What percentage of your conversations are questions and quality listening?

Chapter 5

RESOLUTION

It may be difficult to tie all the pieces of your personal and professional life together in a neat package. Resolution of the many conversations, discussions, and data points that are a routine part of your life is an elusive goal. Personal clarity is critical and absolutely necessary before you are able to effectively lead others with focus and confidence to a resolution with meaningful results. Everyone makes decisions based on their point of view (POV) and this POV has been shaped by their past experience. The emotional impact of their experiences is a major factor.

Plan Your Communication

Think before you speak. You must take into consideration the method, the manner, and the substance of your communication to be successful. Clearly the vision, mission, and goals of any organization should cascade down from the president's office. Research and experience have shown that it is important to have the front line, administrative, and general staff help formulate these issues, in order to increase commitment and motivation. Often, people who are not directly involved or responsible for a particular outcome or project also have good ideas that can contribute to a positive outcome.

The CEO Forum, a diverse group of CEOs that I work with regularly, is a good example of how a person who is not familiar with all the details of another's business is often able to see a completely different, and occasionally superior, solution to a business dilemma. Sometimes a CEO, or possibly even you or I, gets so involved in the details and momentum of business, that she loses site of the big issues. Like the adage goes, she "can't see the forest for the trees."

The CEO Forum has also been very helpful to CEOs who bring issues to be discussed, and choose to be open and honest. Other CEOs are able to ask very poignant questions. Amazingly, the CEO with the issue often realizes that what he thought was an organizational or employee problem was in reality *his* problem. That's good news, because he now personally has control of the solution and can decide to change.

All communication is a two-way process. Every department and person needs unique forms of communication. Let's look at a few of the areas to work on as you plan your future communication.

What You Control

Poor communication is a time waster. People will end up doing the wrong thing or get their feelings hurt, and therefore procrastinate or lose motivation. Finally, when not focused, people spend too much time on what might be called low-payoff activities—specifically, those things that do not directly contribute to bottom line results.

When you plan exactly what you want as a result and how you will communicate the necessary information, you will be able to focus your attention on the other person. This is "getting into the second person." The first person is "me, me, me, and I." When you plan well, you already know your agenda, and all of your senses are looking at the other person.

Now you will be able to perceive if they are listening or not listening. Do they understand? Does their body language indicate they are accepting—"buying in"? Are they under stress? All these things and many more will become apparent to you if you plan well and get "into the second person."

The other person

You don't control other people. As you relate to them, you need to be aware of potential hazards that may interfere with smooth communications. Let's go back to the four primary styles and identify hazards to be avoided when relating to each style.

D Direct Hazards	I Interactive Hazards
Telling them what to do Attacking who they are	Ignoring or rejecting them Negative feedback
S Steady Hazards	C Compliance Hazards
Rushing or confusing them High risks and competition	Criticizing performance Inaccurate information

A positive environment is created by reading and being sensitive to the other person. Once you understand the other person and where she is coming from, you are in a position to help her achieve her goal.

Techniques

A simple yet effective way to test if your message got through is to ask, "What did I say?" or "What do you plan to do?" Remember: Not all people are highly verbal. When you are talking to a reserved and quiet person, you might say, "Show me how you'll fix this" or "Write your plan and show me later."

As a task is proceeding "inspect what you expect." Put a note in your smartphone or digital device to check in with a person to whom you have delegated a task halfway through an assignment. This way, you can keep things on track, you avoid last-minute surprises, and you may give encouragement for a job being done correctly.

Use a communications planner to interface with your most frequently contacted team members. List their names in your smartphone or digital device. Each time you think of something to discuss, write it down next to their name. When you have several items, call them or go to their office. This will save time by minimizing interruptions for you and your team member.

Recently on a long plane ride, I did a fascinating exercise. I mentally went all the way back to the year I was born and listed all the years on a legal pad. Then I put subcategories under each year: family, health, social, school, work, spiritual, and sports. I then recorded what I was able to remember from what happened in my life in each of those years.

We have learned from science in the last few decades that memory is emotion-specific, which means we remember best those things that have a strong emotional component, positive or negative. By doing this exercise, I reflected back on many emotional memories. These emotional events had a high correlation with turning points in my life.

A few examples might help show what I mean. First, a positive experience: When I was 9 years old, I was playing basketball at the school gym on a Saturday morning. I was excited because I had just been elected captain of the team. A woman came to the gym door and asked for me. She was a doctor's wife whose son sang in a quartet with me at church. She said, "David, you have to come with me. We have to get you cleaned up, because you are going to be singing tonight on a TV show." I was first soprano in the boy's quartet. For the next few years, I sang on TV every Saturday. That was the end of my basketball career and the beginning of my singing career.

Now here is a negative experience. When I was in college, I joined the U.S. Navy Reserve to avoid being drafted into the Army. During my second summer in the Navy, I went on a training cruise on the USS *Eversole*, a destroyer. My hammock/rack/bed was in the bowels of the ship with the BTs (boiler tenders), a pretty rough group of guys. I witnessed some very traumatic events. Suffice it to say, when six to eight guys decide to take advantage of a new, young, and insecure sailor, it can get pretty ugly. I am sure you have heard about the way prisoners treat the new young inmates in jail. As a 19-year-old college student, I was shocked and a bit frightened by what I saw. Fortunately, they never targeted me.

This rather emotional experience influenced my decision to leave the Navy and transfer into the U.S. Air Force. In order to get out of the Navy, I went from a two-year reserve commitment in the Navy to almost six years in the Air Force. This required me to go through boot camp twice, once in the Navy and then again in the Air Force. After that, I attended Officer Training School. In all three training environments, I was selected to lead the squadron. The highlight was when we got "honor company." I learned a lot about people, how to lead, and how to work hard and keep focused on the end result. I ultimately became a fighter pilot and logged 208 combat missions in Southeast Asia.

At the time, these experiences seemed to have many negative elements. However, through time, I learned that the adversity made me stronger and turned out for good. I had to go up against the system, face many challenges, and figure out how to maintain a clear vision and focus—a critical skill I mastered when rolling in on a target in a combat situation. It all has helped me learn the value of courageous and creative decision-making.

On the long airplane ride, I went through my entire life, reflecting back on scores of experiences. Then I reviewed and contemplated the patterns I saw. The resolution or result of that exercise was a clear vision of what I want to do with the rest of my life. This book is a direct byproduct.

I encourage you to do this exercise. It is a great way to identify what you really care about, what you are really good at, and what you need to improve. Then you decide how you can best focus your work and energy to have a positive impact on others. As a leader, you will benefit when you encourage and guide your people to examine their strengths, weaknesses, desires, and goals.

Resolution is the last step in our approach to effective communication. Resolution means that a decision has to be made. It may be to agree, disagree, or continue at a later time and date. The more clearly you have defined your intentions, the more easily you will get to resolution in communication. Two of my professional-speaker friends in the National Speakers Association have written books about negotiating. Roger Dawson, in *Secrets of Power Negotiating*, and John Patrick Dolan, in *Negotiate like the Pros*, both advocate striving for a win-win outcome. So do I.

Having been in sales and marketing for decades, I have discovered that much of life is all about selling. To effectively communicate, you have to realize that the other person or groups are trying to sell or influence you, just as you are trying to sell or influence them. When you approach this task in a professional manner, it turns out to be a win-win result. With that framework in mind, let's delve into how to sell from a conceptual point of view. Remember: Your intention is a win-win outcome.

The Art of Asking Questions

"Sellin' ain't tellin', askin' is." I heard this simple but true homily years ago, when working with clients in Texas. Merrill Lynch spent thousands of dollars and six intense months in California and New York City on sophisticated courses and seminars to train me to sell stocks and bonds. Yet, over the years, this bit of country wisdom from Texas has been one of the most powerful and useful lessons I've ever learned. To be successful in sales and in communications, you must master the art of asking questions.

One of the most obvious reasons you ask questions is to acquire information. Let's look at a specific illustration. The conscientious financial advisor will spend a great deal of time and effort to learn about his client. You need all the routine information like name, address, phone number, and past investment experience. But one should look a little deeper.

The person asking questions is always in control of a discussion. This control can be used gracefully to lead and direct the client to a successful outcome, or it can be abused. As a financial professional, I learned it is your responsibility to serve the client in a thorough and ethical manner. The exact same requirement is necessary for an organizational leader. It is impossible to do this if you do not have enough accurate information. Asking many questions needs to be the norm. The most efficient way to get the necessary information is to ask questions.

There is a big difference between efficient and effective communication. Any quality relationship will take time and frequency of interaction. Some executives believe a day of golf is a great way to solidify a new relationship. It's not. Your goal should be frequency of contact. Golf is a very time-intensive, yet infrequent, form of contact. Rather, frequent, short contacts and encounters will build a stronger relationship and make you more memorable to your client. This is the same principle advocated by Ken Blanchard in *The One Minute Manager*.

If you are new in business, a good way to develop this habit is using a checklist. First, you must list all your clients and prospects if you are a financial advisor. If you are an organizational leader, list your key reports, those you report to, vendors, and customers. Then make a list of all the ways you can make contact: phone, e-mail, fax, letter, lunch, appointment, racquetball, golf—the list is endless. Have a simple system to make it easy to use. There are numerous software programs that will help you. Review this list at least weekly to see who you have forgotten, to plan the next mailing campaign, or to benchmark your actual activities to your goals.

How often should you make contact? That depends on the relationship and the nature of your business. Everyone in your database should hear from you at least quarterly. Clients with whom you are trying to develop a relationship may benefit from weekly contact. The main idea is to schedule contacts and monitor/measure those contacts. Clients get very annoyed if they only hear from you when you want to make a sale or collect a check.

Obviously, the goal is to graciously and artfully ask questions during these encounters. No one likes to feel like they are in a deposition. You start with simple, easy-to-answer questions, and then, gradually, the intensity and depth of the questions will escalate. Remember: You are striving to build long-term, profitable relationships. Good quality rapport necessitates some self-disclosure. When you share information about yourself, be sincere and a bit vulnerable.

It is often easier to identify a person's needs as opposed to his or her wants. A financial services professional can easily quantify the necessary insurance needed to pay off the mortgage, bills, and college tuition, and to provide some income for a spouse. But that's the simple part. Wants relate to emotion. This is where you end up practicing psychology without a license. What is really going on in the home with the spouse and children? Are they responsible? Is the business financially stable and growing? Would it be desirable to retire early?

None of these questions is especially profound for the experienced advisor. The real key is to understand how the client *feels* about these issues and the emotional dynamics of the decision-making process. How do you get to this next level of understanding? The answer is asking more questions.

Everybody does everything they do for a reason, either to gain a benefit or avoid a loss. The anonymous benefactor gives gifts because it makes him feel good, worthwhile, or significant. It is said in the legal world that you can solve most white-collar crimes if you can "follow the money." The more advanced your clientele, the more advanced will be their reasons for doing what they do. Even the money-hungry sales type is doing it for more than money. If you don't know why, you just haven't asked the right questions.

Questions are the keys to unlock the vaults of information, needs, wants, and emotions. As you master the art of asking questions, you will gracefully control the discussions with your clients, your colleagues, and your family members.

Who Are You?

It's time to go from preaching to meddling. The most important person you have to question is yourself. Why do you do what you do? What are your motivations? How can you improve? What are your values? Is your behavior consistent with what you say you believe? Those individuals who have integrity achieve the highest levels of success. When required, they are able to survive life's worst traumas. Integrity must be an integral part of a person's career and personal life.

While crossing the North Atlantic, the world famous ocean liner *QE2* was able to endure a rogue wave that measured 95 feet. Captain Ron Warwick, a client and friend, was on the bridge that night. After the event, while he and I were chatting, I asked about that night on the

North Atlantic. When the big wave hit the ship, he said, "It felt like going through a car wash." The ship has integrity and can weather the storm.

As you contemplate your personal integrity, run the following idea through your mind: Person with integrity have clarity, confidence, and definition in three basic areas.

1. They clearly know what they believe, and have defined their beliefs and values ideally in writing.

2. They are able to clearly and concisely communicate these beliefs to others.

3. Their behavior is consistent with these communicated beliefs.

Of course, the best test of this being a reality is the quality and quantity of referrals you receive. As you build relationships with others, are they able to determine your beliefs by how you behave? They don't need to see the "Four Way Test" from your local Rotary club on the wall; they just have to watch and listen to what you do and say. They don't need to have a long explanation about the history and values of your company; they just have to listen to what other people say about you and your reputation. Clients will *trust* a person who they believe has integrity. Without trust, it is impossible to elicit honest feedback from a client.

So Who Cares?

There are at least four groups of people who are critical to your professional development. They are coworkers, centers of influence, vendors, and clients. How much do you care about each of these groups? While writing this, I just received another request from a client. He asked me to meet *pro bono* with a graduate student trying to figure out his future. I have often mentored students, clients' spouses, and others. I love to do it, and it has provided me with a substantial flow of business referrals for many years. For me, it relates to integrity. I know many high-profile business leaders who feel the same way.

Your coworkers are a vital part of your professional team. If you don't have time to show your coworkers that you care about them, in time, they will show you that they don't care about you either. The best way to show interest and concern is to ask them basic questions: What's your name? How was your son's little league game? What's working well for you right now?

The depth and quality of the question you are comfortable asking a co-worker will be a reflection of the quality of your mutual relationship. As you become astute at listening, you will realize how much you can tell about someone by the type of questions they ask. Peter Drucker spent a major part of his time during lectures at Claremont Graduate School, teaching students the value of asking the right question. The depth of the question shows the depth of understanding a person has of a problem.

Financial advisors need to ask questions that make their clients think. A typical question would be "What age do you plan to retire?" Quality questions, on the other hand, would be "Why do you want to retire?" "How will that change your family life?" Why is that important to you?"

When your clients answer these quality questions, you have an opportunity to learn more about their values and beliefs. This information will help you plan how best to serve them. How much money do they really need to retire? What are their emotional drives? How secure is their family situation? What personal connection points can you discover to help induce decisions in the future?

What is the client's attitude toward litigation? Will she sue to make a fast buck? Do you need to closely monitor the contracts you have with this client? All this is useful information. It takes you beyond the competition and helps position you as a true professional.

Centers of influence are those people who respect you and whose position or experiences naturally enable them to send you a continual flow of referrals if you are in sales. By the same token, within an organization, certain people are the primary influencers of others. They are the most valuable kind of marketing and public relations you can ever have. When you ask them questions, it is an opportunity to show your interest and concern for them.

Lots of techniques have been used over the years to try to relate to centers of influence and clients. I remember the insurance agent who would give a statue and plaque to celebrate a client's newborn child. We've all sent out newspaper articles of interest, birthday cards, neckties, or a special bottle from a trip abroad. These may all be very sincere gestures. However, none are as sincere as the well-thought-out question and your undivided attention as you genuinely listen to the answer. This is an investment of your time with another person—not on the golf course, but rather by practicing frequency of contact.

Communication is just like sales in another way. Many people think that there is a secret to memorizing the super "closing" question. They also think it takes a lot of courage to close. Nothing could be further from the truth. If you are a real pro at selling or a master at communicating, you know that it is a dance—a continual process. Think of it as driving a car and honoring road signs and traffic lights. You proceed when you have a green light. A smile, a forward nodding of the head, and a relaxed manner indicate to you that the other person is giving you a green light.

Dramatic moves observed in body language, facial grimaces, and confused looks or objections to what you are saying all mean a red light. That means stop, back up, and excuse yourself to fight on another day. When people say no, it is often because they either don't understand, or they want help in understanding or personalizing something you already said. People say yes and no with their eyes a lot more than by actually saying the words.

With practice and sensitivity developed through a period of time, you will be able to recognize the yellow lights. That's when you can see you have to slow down, become more patient and gentle, or prepare to stop.

Learning how and when to ask the right question to get resolution is definitely an art form. It takes time, training, and lots of practice. As Martin Luther King, Jr., said, "People don't get along because they fear each other. People fear each other because they don't know each other. They don't know each other because they have not properly communicated with each other."[1]

Take Time to Reflect

As you contemplate this chapter, take a few minutes alone and answer these questions.

1. Do you think before you speak?

2. How do you ensure that you are not offending others and avoiding the typical hazards?

3. Have you identified the learning style of each of your direct reports?

4. When you think about your life's turning points, what have you learned?

5. Will you build a list of all your key constituents, vendors, customers, and so on. and their communication preferences? Why might this be important?

6. What are you doing to improve your ability in the art of asking questions?

7. Can you think of any unique ways to get to know people better?

PART II

EXECUTION

Are you striving for success or significance? Both success and significance necessitate living life based on predetermined, worthwhile, personal values. Success often relates to the accumulation of possessions with goals of "having." Significance is all about impact and influence, with goals of "becoming." As Erich Fromm says in his seminal work, *To Have or to Be?*, "Joy comes from giving and sharing, not from hoarding and exploiting."[1]

Goals based on your clearly defined values need to be translated into a specific strategy and then broken down into a practical plan of action. Plans are useless if not acted upon. As Peter Drucker said, "Plans are only good intentions unless they immediately degenerate into hard work." That hard work must be focused, effective, and consistent. To master execution, it is necessary for you to develop certain habits. In the words of Aristotle, "We are what we repeatedly do. Excellence, then, is not an act but a habit."[2]

You are about to discover a foolproof method to ensure progress. The Cycle of Success is a core concept within *The CEO Code*. First, we explore a proven and practical formula for setting goals and how to structure them so they are positive and enabling. Once your goals are established and written down, it is time to focus on taking deliberate action and implementing practical tactics to ensure completion both by you and others.

Positive action needs to be repeated again and again. You will then develop new habits. Your new habits will impact your thinking, and in time you will create new attitudes. Your attitudes will then influence the way you feel. The Cycle of Success will act as a crank or generator for you to continue setting goals and achieving more.

Fundamentally, you can categorize all that you do as a CEO or leader into four basic activities: planning, communicating, managing, and executing. Companies that have a leader who understands which of these four is most important, and allocates time accordingly, have a clear advantage over those that don't. You have probably heard it suggested that the smart executive will work *on* their business more than they work *in* their business. Many leaders are so busy trying to go faster and faster that they don't realize they need a better plan with a clear focus. They are merely chasing their own tail, as opposed to moving forward deliberately to a specific objective.

Another fundamental dilemma you might wrestle with is the difference between effectiveness and efficiency. There is a time for both; however, it is important to know the difference between the two and to understand when one or the other is necessary. As Peter Drucker writes, "Doing the right thing—even if not perfectly executed—is far superior to perfectly executing the wrong thing."[3]

This part of *The CEO Code* is all about getting the right things done in a timely manner and will be very useful to you. You will see how to master the core of your business, how to take control of the daily flow of your career, and how to have a blueprint to execute your master plan.

Chapter 6

Action

One of my favorite affirmations is "I do it now or write it down." All of my clients are given a 3 × 5 card with this affirmation written on it to be used as a reminder. You will see it pinned to their bulletin boards or on their desk, and they are always asking for extras to give to their people. This habit helps ensure that nothing will fall through the cracks.

Writing things down is important. During a seminar, one of my clients shared a cute saying: "The shortest pencil is longer than the longest memory." The added bonus to writing things down is that you have peace of mind, because you are not trying to remember a treasure trove of trivia. Your mind becomes free to create, plan, and complete high-priority tasks that advance your journey toward building your masterpiece.

The words *write* and *pencil* are Old English, before computers, metaphors for key strokes when used to input data on devices like smartphones. It is imperative that you continually stay abreast of the latest developments in technology. As Moore's Law has taught us many years ago, computer hardware capability doubles every two years. This is a moving target; rest and you will fall behind.

There is one caveat. On any given day, there are a myriad ideas and tasks you will write down as notes, lists, and reminders. Maybe you use a Day-Timer or appointment book, whereas others use a smartphone. Some prefer Post-its, envelopes, and random pieces of paper for lists and reminders. I highly recommend that you keep all planning, note-taking, and action plans in one central place. If you are using technology tools to assist you, don't forget to back up and save your information.

I am reminded of the late John Wooden, the remarkable basketball coach for UCLA. His teams won 10 NCAA national championships over a 12-year period. The way he would start each new team every year was always the same. He had them all sit down and, in a kind but very deliberate manner, he taught them how to put on their socks and tie their basketball shoes. This coaching ritual was not so different from that of Vince Lombardi, the winning coach of two Super Bowls and six NFL National Championships. He would stand up in front of all his players at the first practice of each football season and declare, with the ball held high, "Gentlemen, this is a football." So, now let's get into the why, what, and how of taking action!

Values

The foundation for your goals and activities is based on clarifying your values. Your personal life and your professional life will be most fulfilling when the basis of all your actions, activities, and decisions is grounded in your values. Unfortunately, many people have not taken the time to clearly define their values. A CEO or leader must develop the ability to make good decisions. When you make decisions based on values, there is a high probability of having integrity and congruence. This leads to better decision-making.

If you don't have a list of your values, take some time to list and prioritize them the same way you probably invest time to establish a strategic plan for your business. A healthy and vibrant company is one that has clearly defined values and communicates them to all employees.

When the leader's values and goals are consistent with the organization's values and goals, we see integrity. Integrity leads to strength and clear focus; it is a worthwhile objective. High integrity is evident when a person or organization has the quality of being honest, upholds high moral standards, and behaves consistently.

With low integrity, there are huge problems. When people know what the leader says his or her values and goals are, and then observe that same leader violating those values or ignoring the goals, they lose faith. The leader's behavior destroys focus and compromises the cultural strength and resilience of the organization.

How do you best share values and teach decision-making? The best way is not to share your values verbally or in writing with your employees or your children. Rather, they will learn by watching you. They will be watching your actions, activities, and decisions. Based on what they see you do, they will know what your values are. The same is true of your goals. Based on your behavior, people will know your goals. You will discuss and write your goals, but never forget that your behavior is preeminent.

Your own current goals can easily be defined. Start by taking an inventory of how you spend your time and your money. It will become readily apparent what your personal goals are. You will have clarity when you have a written list of your values and your goals. Be sure that the written list is consistent with the way you invest your time and your money. Essentially you want to do a gap analysis between your actual use of time and money, versus the way you ideally would invest your time and money if you were closely following your values and goals. What is the difference between where you are and where you want to go? This method of assessment also needs to be taught to your employees at every level of the organization.

Goals

Goals lead directly to action. Fundamentally, it is critical that you and your employees clearly know the difference between effective and efficient behaviors, goals, and actions. Effective means doing the right or the important things that produce results. Efficient is doing a task in a competent and businesslike manner. Too often people focus on doing something a certain way (efficient) rather than considering how valuable their activity is (effective). I'll never forget a particular young coworker at Merrill Lynch. He was a well-organized and knowledgeable broker who sat a few desks ahead of me. I marveled at how organized he was. The problem was he spent most of his time organizing and sorting leads, rather than contacting clients and making sales calls. He was fired!

In the business environment, there must be a blending of the goals of each individual and those of the organization. People have a desire to be successful and so do organizations. If there is a lack of success by either, the individual or the organization, then the place to start making improvements is in the clarity of the goals. The goals and activities used to get you to a certain point may not be good enough to keep you productive and profitable, let alone get you to where you need to be.

Think in terms of continuous improvement. You want to be constantly on the lookout for new and better ways to accomplish things. Have a mindset of always evaluating and striving to do it better. Measure yourself and maintain gradual, but constant, improvement.

Goals determine the results. In fact, the results are merely a reflection of the actual, though not always stated, goals. Therefore, when you closely examine a person's or organization's results, it will give you insight into what their *real* goals are. Identify what the person or organization pays attention to. What they say is not as important as what they do. Watch what a person pays attention to, and you can tell what his or her unconscious intention is.

Many times we see organizations or bosses arbitrarily trying to set goals for their employees. This is ultimately a futile exercise. The only goals you or anyone else will get really excited about are your own. Every worthwhile goal has to be one that gives you something that you personally care about having or being. A good leader will spend a considerable amount of time coaching employees and working with people to make sure they understand why and how a particular goal is important to the organization, and exactly how that goal will benefit the employee. The benefit must relate to the values and emotions that the employee cares about personally. If this isn't being done in your group, ask questions: Why are we doing this? What is our endgame? How will we know when we have achieved our goal?

John and I were college classmates. John and I both joined the Air Force and flew fighters. John decided to make it a career and became a very successful lieutenant colonel in the USAF. His OERs (Officer Effectiveness Reports), were superb. The U.S. Air Force looks at the level of competence and then asks for the evaluating officer to rank the candidate as to promotability ahead of or with peers. John was a great fighter pilot and also had demonstrated his ability to manage, execute, and complete all assignments, and was recommended to be promoted ahead of his peers. He was dedicated and ranked "superior."

As he was completing a tour of duty at the Pentagon, his commander discussed his next assignment. It would probably be overseas and in a remote area; this was designed to balance his resume and ensure his next promotion, assuming he did a quality job. His family would stay behind in the United States.

Unfortunately, John had some personal issues with his youngest son and felt it important that he stay stateside so he could be home to spend time with his family. His boss was disappointed and explained that if he didn't take the suggested assignment, it would not reflect kindly on his career. John chose to stay in the United States, and with that decision realized that it was time for him to make plans for his next career. The military was now a dead end for his future. It would be very unlikely he would ever be promoted to colonel.

Big companies sometimes operate the same way. The needs of the company come before the needs of a specific employee's family. I have seen this in large professional services firms, technology companies, and manufacturing companies. I am sure you have seen the same scenario or even been a participant in this cycle of events.

Some companies are realizing how important it is to take a holistic approach to the development of their employees and are reaping great rewards in the form of loyalty, dedication, and productive results. The key here is to be sure your values and the values of your company are in alignment. As a leader, it is incumbent upon you to clearly communicate the goals of the organization and be sure that the employee's goals are in synch with the organization. The basis of these goals has to be value-driven. The organization and individual must be a good match.

To help you structure an effective goals program, let's review some basic concepts. First and foremost, be sure the goal is stated in positive terms, as opposed to negative terms. The classic New Year's resolutions are a good example of negative goals: I am going to stop smoking. I am going to lose weight. I am going to stop interrupting people.

These may all be worthwhile goals. However, let's think about it for a minute. Each one is asking you to stop or lose something. In a very real psychological sense, you will be deprived of doing something you have enjoyed, or at least give up some developed habits that have resulted in pleasure or satisfaction. You are trying to conquer or achieve your goal by using self-discipline—a noble task.

Let me ask you a few simple questions. Which is a stronger force for you when you consider your behavior: self-discipline or your imagination? Do advertisers try and appeal to your self-discipline or your imagination? Why do they put beautiful girls in automobile advertisements? How about piles of gold coins in ads to entice you to buy gold? They do it because it works.

Disney is a good example of a company that understands the power of imagination. They have very deliberately built an entire culture around creating a fantasy experience. Everything and everybody is part of the show. No one has a job in the traditional sense; their employees are "cast members," and most importantly, their revenue comes from creatively entertaining their "guests" (customers).

If this is all true, as I believe it is, how do we take advantage of this reality when setting goals? Simple: We state them in *positive* terms. Negative goals are not able to create the imagination, desire, and results that positive ones can. There is amazing power to be harnessed when you empower your imagination. Can you imagine all of your staff really enthusiastic and excited to achieve their goals? How about having all those goals clearly aligned with your company's goals for sales, profits, and cash flow? Are you starting to get the picture?

Let's review a proven formula (SSMARTT) that will help you set worthwhile goals. Each letter in SSMARTT stands for an element that is important to formulating a goal: S = self, S = specific, M = measurable, A = attainable, R = realistic, T = tangible, T = target date.

The first key to setting a goal is *self*. Why do you want to achieve this goal? Do you see what's in it for you? Do you have enough authority and responsibility? Does it engage you emotionally? When your *why* is big, your goals can be big. If there is no *why*, there will be no motivation.

There are many possible dimensions to how a person can see what's in it for them. Sometimes it is as simple as a monetary reward. More likely, it will have an emotional component that may relate to pride, being part of the team, or just wanting to be the best. When you think of the military, it is hard to believe they are serving for the money. Sometimes it is directly related to job security or obligations to family or others. Everyone has a different reason they want a particular goal. As a leader, it is important that you recognize this and help each person personalize the reason so that he or she is motivated. One thing is certain: They are not doing it for you or just because you tell them to do it.

Nothing becomes dynamic until it first becomes *specific*. This is the next key to setting a goal. You must be specific. Who? What? Where? When? Why? Be sure you use numbers wherever possible.

Let's pause for a moment. Look at the lights in your office. Is it diffused light? Can you feel any heat? Think what you could do if you used a laser beam. It's also light, but it can cut through steel, be used in eye surgery, or help you precisely aim a weapon. The difference is the light of a laser is focused and specific. Specific goals become dynamic.

If you can't *measure* it you can't manage it. Every goal needs to be measured. The best way to do this is with numbers on a chart in plain view. This will then show you where you've been, where you are now, and where you are going.

Any goal that is important must be measured. Measurement is a form of feedback and a way to keep current on the status of progress or lack of it. The measurement should be frequent, and monitored and recorded by the person striving to achieve the goal. Many times I have seen situations in which someone else is keeping the measurement for the person charged with the goal. Invariably, this leads to misunderstanding, or it generates excuses as to why the goal is not being achieved. There is a much higher level of emotional involvement when someone is keeping score on him- or herself and is displaying the results for others to see. Those who resist measurement often are resisting the scorekeeping, because they either don't want the goal or are afraid they can't achieve it.

Attainable goals are the ones you believe you can achieve. One good reason to keep charts, measurements, and records is so you have a frame of reference for future goals. Your past experience has a big influence on your belief system.

We learn new things by making a reference or correlation to things we have experienced in the past. Remember the Superman movie? People saw this flying object going across the sky and said, "It's a bird. It's a plane. It's Superman!" All learning is a building process. The same is true for what we believe is possible to attain. People who have a wealth of experience with computers love to try new technology. Have you noticed how people who are "technologically challenged" avoid trying new computers and devices? Past experience is important, and keeping a record of past achievements is equally important. By doing so, you can set up goals you can realistically attain in the future.

Do you have a bucket list? I do, and I also keep track of things I feel are noteworthy that I have achieved. Whenever I feel down or a bit depressed, I review my list of accomplished goals, and it revitalizes me and pumps my adrenaline.

Every goal will take time, effort, knowledge, maybe money, and probably many other resources. Be sure you have the resources to achieve a goal that is *realistic*. Sometimes it is necessary to back up and set a different goal to acquire a basic resource before you go for the big goal.

When you set several small goals and are able to check them off, it gives you a feeling of accomplishment. This will then build your confidence, and you will be excited to set more goals. Goals can be *tangible* or intangible. However, it will be easier to measure and chart them if you are able to convert the intangible goals into tangible ones. This takes a bit of creativity.

Suppose your goal is to become more gregarious. Arguably, that is pretty intangible. Let's convert that same goal into something tangible.

Start by setting a simple goal such as saying hello to two people a day. The next one might be to say hello and smile. Then progress to say hello, smile, and shake hands. All these simple tangible steps to the goal can easily be measured and charted.

Last but not least, you want to set a *target date* for completion of the goal. Until the target date is set, it is just a dream or a wish. When you have defined and thought out exactly what your goal is using this formula and believe you can achieve it, it will be easy to write one and set a target date. Now let's hit it!

Action

Execution is the key—to paraphrase Peter Drucker, "Everything must degenerate into work if anything is to happen."[1] Remember: This is all based on having a clear picture of your prioritized values and goals before you take action.

There are three very specific tools or techniques that have helped many of my executive and CEO clients get more of the important things done. The first is having a very practical vision of what action you need to take in the form of an Ideal Week. The second is to effectively use charts and graphs. And the third is to understand how to design and use Key Function Indicators, KFIs.

Once you have set the goal, you need to take action, even if you don't feel like it. That means you must overcome fear, fatigue, and nervousness. If you decide to do or not do something simply because of the way you feel, you will end up in a negative spiral downward. If your values are worthwhile and your *why* is big enough, you will muster the internal courage to take action.

Ideal Week

You've heard it said that a picture is worth a thousand words. What this means to you is that when you work with pictures, you see and relate at an entirely different and more comprehensive level than you do with just words. It is amazing how once you clarify your truly high-payoff activities and get them properly placed in an Ideal Week, your productivity goes up dramatically.

The place to start is to identify your high-payoff activities. These are the activities that create the most impact or result toward your vision and goals. This can be a simple list. You will find that all of your activities can be categorized into four basic areas: planning, communicating, managing, and executing. The higher your functional responsibility in an organization, the more time you will spend in planning and communicating. The closer you are to the front line functions of an organization, the more time you will spend on executing or supervisory functions.

A point of clarification: we are using the term *action* to mean you *do a specific thing*. *Execution* relates to the process of implementation. The receptionist answering the phone equals action. The salesperson writing up an order equals action. The accountant working on a spreadsheet equals action. Execution is a broader concept and includes many actions used to carry out or put into effect a plan.

One of the best ways to determine your list of actions is to take an inventory of your daily activities. This is easy to do. Keep a piece of paper on the corner of your desk, and every 15 minutes, jot down what you are doing. Once you have the list of activities, use hash marks to indicate time spent on each activity. After a day of work, review the list and your hash marks, and group or categorize the activities. Finally, differentiate between the high-payoff and low-payoff activities.

Undoubtedly you have both high-payoff and low-payoff activities. Planning is clearly your highest-payoff activity, whether you are the CEO or the receptionist. Communication is next in order of importance, because the best-laid plans of mice and men are useless if not properly communicated. Then comes managing, which includes scheduling, evaluating, controlling, and similar supervisory activities. Last on the list is the execution of the types of activities previously mentioned: phone, writing orders, crunching numbers in a spread sheet, and so on.

Many other activities fill the typical day. Several are obviously in the low-payoff column. Let's list a few of the low payoffs: coffee breaks, driving, water cooler chats, reading the paper, and browsing the Internet.

I was recently doing some training in the Chicago executive office of a Fortune 500 company and was waiting in the training room between sessions. I happened to notice a fellow sitting in the typical corporate cubicle just across the hall from the training room. His right hand was on his mouse but not moving. He was facing the corner so that from behind, where I was, his head and neck appeared to be the same diameter. I noticed this because he was silhouetted against four large computer screens on his wraparound desk. There was no movement. Then suddenly his head jerked to the side; then another long period of no movement. He was literally asleep at the switch. This is the ultimate low-payoff activity. I would not share this story if it was not completely true, and had I not seen this basic scenario in several other organizations over the years.

As a leader you need to *plan* to *communicate* with your people by walking around. Peter Drucker often reminded his clients and students how important it was to MBWA (*m*anage *b*y *w*alking *a*round). In class, he told the story of how Alfred Sloan, CEO and Chairman of General Motors, built the world's largest corporation, and yet would go undercover to dealerships and factories to see what was really going on, with the aim of improving performance and results. The 21st-century version of this is the Emmy-winning, international reality show, *Undercover Boss*.

Planning will ideally be done twice every day: early morning and end of day. This is different than the intense efforts at annual or quarterly strategic planning sessions. Strategic plans are very important and should be done regularly. I do this and have facilitated scores of strategic planning sessions, weekend retreats, and plan reviews for clients. The purpose of the Ideal Week is to make those strategic plans come off the bookshelf or hard drive in your computer, and have the activities boiled down to daily and weekly activities. (There is a sample Ideal Week on page 213 in Appendix I.)

Self-discipline

Let's look at discipline for a moment. A discipline is an activity in which you can engage now that will enable you to ultimately do something that you are not capable of doing currently. Running is a good illustration. At first it is difficult to run a mile if you haven't ever tried. However, with a gradual program of pushing your limits, in time you can easily run a mile. The dictionary says discipline is "training intended to produce a specified character or pattern of behavior."

Three simple disciplines that will help you use your smartphone or other digital device effectively are to-do list, blocking time, and hash marks. Each of these are easy to do, but will have a huge impact on your ability to follow through and control your priorities. Focus these three disciplines on the critical few high-payoff activities that produce results.

To-do list

I suggest you create and record your To Do List in one central book or digital device at the end of each day before you leave work, while your mind is still focused. Then carry the book or device with you at all times: at home, to lunch, in the car—I mean everywhere. Whenever an idea hits, *write it down*. Then review the to-do list first thing in the morning and prioritize it. One good way is: A = must do today; B = imperative but not urgent; C = important to do soon. The last thing is to number the items in each category and transfer or cut and paste the letter and number to your schedule. Thus, A-1 at 9 a.m.; A-2 at lunchtime; B-1 on the way home.

Blocking time

Now you are ready to block time for all of your planned activities. By "activities," I mean appointments, meetings, lunch, exercise, phone calls, correspondence, planning time, writing reports, or preparing bids. Obviously, this is just a sample of the kinds of activities you can group together and plan to do at a specific time. Blocking time and grouping activities has many benefits. It helps you to focus, it minimizes interruptions, and it forces you to plan ahead. Can you think of other benefits?

Hash marks

The third discipline I suggest is to use hash marks, just some simple lines, to indicate transportation time. This is another form of blocking time to be done in your book or smartphone. Often we think of a meeting as lasting one hour. However, when you put hash marks before and after the meeting for transportation time required, you realize it really cost you two hours to attend the one-hour meeting. Make sure your plan is flexible and has some open time for the unexpected. You now have a picture of your day and can change it if you don't like what you see.

Charts and Graphs

Charts and graphs are especially valuable for monitoring high-payoff activities, as well as your progress toward personal or organizational goals. Good charts give you a perspective that is far more beneficial than pages of data from a computer. A chart shows you, in a clear and simple way, where you have been, where you are right now, and where you are going. Charts will elicit emotional involvement better than a stack of computer data sheets. Yet, the precise performance measurement is often distilled from these data sheets. You need to get it out of the stack of paper and on to a relevant and current chart.

Charts are most useful when they are hung on a wall in a highly visible spot. Entries should be made by the person responsible for performing the task being measured. Pay particular attention to the trends that the chart shows. That way, you can catch exceptions before they become a crisis. Ideally, every person in an organization will have a performance chart that shows if they "win" or "lose" each day based on a measure (KFI, Key Function Indicator) that directly relates to the organization's primary goals.

If you are managing by walking around, it is very easy to glance at the chart on the wall at every person's work station, whether it is a desk or a machine on the shop floor, and understand how things are going. Are they exceeding expectations, right on target, or falling behind? This is the opportune time to apply Ken Blanchard's three key ideas from the *One Minute Manager*: set goals, praise, or reprimand.

If you reprimand someone for an error or for falling behind, remember that he will have to be built back up emotionally. The amount and frequency of giving praise to rebuild your team members will depend on the individual, but a common rule of thumb is 4 × 1—that's four praises or positive comments for each negative one. Some people think this idea is crazy. They think people need to "get a life" and do what they are told. Well, that's not reality today. If you feel that way, you might want to go back and review Chapter 3. Thomas S. Monson said it well: "When performance is measured, performance improves. When performance is measured and reported, the rate of improvement accelerates."[2]

KFIs (Key Function Indicators)

If you can't measure it, you can't manage it. Technology has given us the incredible ability to measure virtually everything. However, those measurements are useless unless they are examined, evaluated, and used to provide a context for continuous improvement and adjustments. The concept of using KFIs is to pick out the critical few things that must be closely monitored to have the maximum impact on results. Companies often pay particular attention to a few critical organizational metrics:

- ▶ ROI (Return on investment).
- ▶ EBITDA (Earnings before interest, taxes, depreciation and amortization).
- ▶ Market share.
- ▶ Cash flow.

For monitoring and improving job performance, it is highly recommended that a few KFIs are recorded daily on a chart that is displayed on the wall at the employee's work station. For personal improvement, you might want to record your performance on your smartphone or in your book. There are all kinds of unique smartphone applications that you can use to measure everything from food intake or exercise, to communication and comprehensive CRM (customer relationship management).

Computerized dashboards are becoming more common and popular. Several of my clients have designed customized dashboards for their business. They are able to measure activities, finances, and bank balances on a real-time basis. One of the more unique apps a client developed was for seniors who were in nursing homes. On a real-time basis, they are able to measure when and who gave the residents medications, how often they were checked on by staff, meals served and what was eaten, and doctor visits and results. All this was available with live videos and data in real-time on the Internet. Children can remotely check on their parents in the nursing home any time of the day, giving them greater peace of mind. The only limitation to how you set up your KFIs is your imagination.

KFIs should measure the things you deem important. How do they relate to your personal and organizational goals? If you wish to increase the level of trust your people have in you, break down your efforts into simple, specific actions. For example, measure how much you listen to your employees or compliment a person's good work. This is similar to the Boy Scout's "good deed of the day." If you are concerned with maintaining relationships with employees, clients, or vendors, set up a KFI to help you focus on this task. For example, it can measure the number of times per day you speak to someone, with no agenda other than to find out how she is doing in her personal life.

When focusing on production or results, you may want to have a KFI for how many new people you contact about business opportunities, or how often you recognize a salesperson who has landed a big contract. You can even schedule a small celebration and share sincere thanks for a job well done. Imagine what would happen on a long-term basis in your organization if you had a goal of finding at least one person in the office each day who you "catch doing something right" and you focused on saying "thank you." You can totally change the culture of your organization! It will take time, but it all starts when you have prioritized your values, structured clearly defined goals, and then committed to taking *action*. By having a chart, using daily measurements, and creating an Ideal Week to give a framework to your activities, you will find your efforts will reap great rewards and impact all the people who are watching your behavior.

A leading partner in a major accounting firm started to monitor the time he spent talking to his teenage son about how his son's life was going, with no other predetermined agenda. I was blown away during one of our coaching sessions when he stopped talking, started to get emotional, and his eyes welled up with tears. He then said, "Dave, my wife told me about a conversation she had with our son this week. He told her 'Dad has changed. What's going on? I think he really loves me.'"

Take Time to Reflect

As you contemplate this chapter, take a few minutes alone and answer these questions.

1. What is your specific plan to stay current on technological developments?

2. How do you centralize and control your to-do list and other items that need attention?

3. Have you written down a prioritized list of your values?

4. Do you have a notebook, computer app, or system to record and monitor your goals?

5. If your Ideal Week is a picture of your life, how can you make it more beautiful?

6. How do you measure each day to know if you win or lose?

7. When people watch your behavior do they clearly see your values and goals?

Chapter 7

Repetition

Much of human behavior is unconscious. When this trait is combined with the way we make decisions, a process based on need fulfillment and emotional triggers, it becomes clear that to change how we behave is not a simple matter. It all starts by knowing what is important to do, and repeating it, as opposed to what should be stopped or avoided.

Self-awareness at this level is uncommon. You and I have certain behaviors or habits that we are not aware of, and some of those behaviors may even be negative or destructive. That state or condition is called being "unconsciously incompetent." In a very real sense, this is a form of ignorance—not stupidity, just the condition of being unaware.

Actor John Goodman was interviewed on *CBS Sunday Morning* recently and discussed how his life has changed since he stopped drinking alcohol. He moved and now lives in New Orleans. "Yeah, let the demons chase me, and they can knock all they want. I'm not home," Goodman laughed. "I'm learning the important things in life, which are petting my dogs, saying hi to my wife, looking at this beautiful city. Little things that I just missed or I just slept through for 30 years."[1] For Goodman, the condition of being unaware was exacerbated by drinking.

When you develop keen awareness of self, it enables you to make the necessary adjustments to modify or change the outcomes that you manifest. This can directly relate to your relationships, your ability to produce results, and your feelings of satisfaction and accomplishment.

The High Achiever's Guide to Happiness by Vance and Carol Ann Caesar is based on doctoral research done by Vance. They found that high achievers have high drive, high responsibility, high confidence, and low self-esteem. His study found that 92 percent rated themselves with some degree of unhappiness. Based on my mentoring and coaching experience, this is a valid finding. One of the biggest problems is that the executive is often unaware of those things he or she repeats unconsciously, behaviors that are unintentionally leading them to significant dissatisfaction, difficulty in relationships, and lack of quality, balanced results.

General David Petraeus, the highly respected and decorated warrior, was forced to resign as director of the Central Intelligence Agency because of an illicit affair. Both General Petraeus and Paula Broadwell, his mistress, were intelligent, gifted, and high-achieving individuals. Their high-profile tragedy was several years in developing. They first met at Harvard, where she was a graduate student when the general was invited to the university to give a lecture. A friendship began as a result of this chance meeting, both being graduates of the United States Military Academy at West Point and having many additional things in common. One can only wonder what behaviors they exhibited that originally seemed to be innocent and normal, but gradually developed into an attraction where both individuals compromised their values.

You can never totally let your guard down. You must be constantly vigilant if you desire to achieve great things. Clearly define your values and constantly, on a daily basis, review and reinforce them. This is just as true for you as an individual as it is for your organization.

In the previous chapter, we clarified the goal-setting process and how it needs to be grounded in your values. Then we discussed several ideas to help you take action. Having an Ideal Week, using charts, and practicing self-measurement are very practical and useful tools. Now that we have defined a specific action, we will discuss how and why we repeat it.

As it states in Proverbs 23:7, "As a man thinketh in his heart, so is he."[2] In a very practical way, if you believe this, you realize that those things that you are doing are a manifestation of your thoughts. However, there are many things you don't consciously think about; you just do them. Examples of this are easy to identify. When you take a shower, do you automatically follow the same pattern of applying soap or drying yourself? I always start washing and then drying my head first, then my arms, and so forth. When you pull your car out of the garage, do you automatically push the button to close the door? I have actually had to drive around the block and come back to the house to be sure I actually closed the door.

Do you automatically listen and then pause before you respond to someone in a conversation? This may be hard for you to do, especially if you have already developed a habit of interrupting people. Think of the many nuances of communications discussed in Part I of this book. What are the behaviors you repeat unconsciously?

My business of mentoring and coaching executives is designed to help identify those things they need to stop doing and helping them start doing things that will advance their goals. Most often, my clients are aware that they can do better. They want different and better results than they are currently getting. Naturally, they are not aware of some of the things they are doing unconsciously that are hindering their progress. The various levels of unconscious incompetence may be very subtle.

Many of my clients are very bright, well-educated, and financially very successful. Yet, I am continually amazed how often they are not aware of the effect or impact they have on other people. Three groups that conspicuously demonstrate this, based on my experience, are physicians, attorneys, and accountants. Whether it is the physician who lacks a caring bedside manner and has what nurses call the "god" complex, or the attorney who thinks she is always right and won't consider the view of others, or the accountant who believes he cannot make a mistake because he is good with the numbers, all these people are unaware of how their unconscious behaviors cause others to suffer.

On the other hand, based on my observation of clients, those individuals who understand how to effectively relate to other people have consistently been the most successful, based on earnings and status, within their organization or their industry. They have also experienced the most enduring and happiest marriages.

A Fortune 500 company that I worked with several years ago tasked one of its divisions to reduce payroll. This was a manufacturing company with several thousand employees. For more than a year, I had been working with the division's CEO and executive team. It was fascinating to witness the decision process the CEO went through to make the final cut of one of his direct reports. It was not based on measurable results, because all were doing a good job. Neither was it based on longevity or work load. The final cut was made because the individual wasn't the best team player. Bear in mind, he was a good guy, and his department made a good and significant contribution to the bottom line; he just was not liked by everyone. (Similarly, Scott Forstall, senior vice president of Apple, was recently fired for "persistent personality clashes with other key executives" and dismal results from the new Apple maps application, which he managed.) This is just a reality of the way people behave and make decisions. I am not trying to say it is right or wrong. It is what it is—reality.

What can we learn from these stories? You must work on your competence and results for any organization. However, given that you are highly competent and you work with very competent colleagues, it is incumbent upon you to master the art of people relationships. Your ability to effectively relate to others can often be the critical factor in a client's or boss's decision to hire or fire you. So let's work on how we can improve ourselves and learn to repeat behavior that enhances our chances of winning.

There are three specific things you can do to become more aware of yourself. The first is to ask for feedback. After every meeting, sales call, or conversation, ask for feedback. There are many creative ways to do this, including asking, "How did I do? How could this meeting have been handled better? What would you recommend I say next time I am in this kind of situation?"

Second, you can get other people to formally give you input on your performance by conducting a formal or informal 360 review. This type of review means you get input from everyone around you: coworkers, boss, clients, vendors, family, and so on. An easy way to start this process is to request people to *share anonymously in writing* your three biggest strengths and what three things you need to improve. I first started doing this as a young broker with Merrill Lynch; it was and is invaluable. Once you get the results, throw out the top and bottom, the best and worst, responses, and look for patterns within the rest of the input. Some people love you and love is blind, causing them to give glowing feedback. Others have had a bad experience with you, and they can't let it go, or maybe they have issues of their own; this may also skew their opinion disproportionally. Resist attachment to one particular comment; rather, focus on trends and patterns.

Your third choice is to get a coach or mentor who can not only facilitate the 360 process, but also guide you into ways to change and improve. Choose wisely in this arena. It is possible for virtually anyone to call themselves a coach. Unfortunately, most certifications and approvals are not very rigorous. There are many profligate professional accreditations that are proffered merely to appropriate fees from naive beginning coaches. Thus, *caveat emptor*—let the buyer beware.

A comprehensive 360 assessment process brings you to the next level; you are no longer unaware or unconscious of the nuances of your behavior. You have now become conscious of your incompetence. Voila!

So let's move on to the behavior that you need to repeat. You will benefit from using some practical tools to help you remember to repeat doing certain things. Tie a string around your finger, put a Post-it on your computer, start a checklist, or ask someone to remind you or hold you accountable. You might also get some input on how to apply your new actions and tell others what you intend to do in the future. This form of sharing will get your ego and reputation involved, so it might be a little tough to do. However, it is a useful and practical way to encourage your desired behavior by setting yourself up for social pressure from friends or colleagues. With practice, you will be able to actually do the new action. Let's say you have decided to stop interrupting people. The key is to convert it into a positive action—listening—and repeat the effort over and over again.

An additional tool or technique for you at this point is to use an affirmation. An affirmation is simply a declarative statement—in the first person, present tense—which proclaims a fact or condition that you aspire to achieving. It is a way to talk to yourself, and with repetition, it will start to influence your thoughts and at some point your beliefs and actions. Remember: We have the ability to literally rewire our brain. Take control of how your brain develops; this is a much better alternative than letting the media shape your thoughts. Jealously guard what you allow your mind to focus on, and make it productive and positive. Let me share a few simple examples of an affirmation: I do it now or write it down. I feel healthy; I feel happy; I feel terrific. I focus on one goal at a time.

Unfortunately, many people allow negative affirmations and thoughts to tarnish their mind and results. Here are a few examples: I don't trust anyone. The only time something is done right is when I do it myself. I can't seem to ever get anything right.

Bear in mind that you are working with your internal locus of control when you talk to yourself and set goals that are based on your values. There are also many influences from the outside that can affect your repetition of certain actions that are necessary to achieve your goals. The single biggest influence is the people you choose to hang out with socially and at work. It goes back to the old adages "Birds of a feather flock together," and "Show me your friends and I'll tell you who you are." There is no reason you can't become very deliberate about who your friends are and the people with whom you associate. They will all have some influence on you, good or bad. It is your decision.

As you go through this process of setting goals, taking action, and repeating those actions, you will discover that you will develop "conscious competence." This means being aware of what you want to do, trying it, and gradually becoming good at it.

The University of California–Irvine has done significant research on the brain and memory. I remember the first seminar I attended there several years ago during which James L. McGaugh, professor and author, said that we realize there is much more that we don't know about memory and the brain than we do know.

Joseph LeDoux, in his book *Synaptic Self*, discusses how our brains become who we are. Let's paraphrase and review a few of the main points he discusses in his book. We know that our brain is made up of several systems; in a sense, each is its own computer. The systems work together to accomplish tasks like parallel computers, as opposed to your PC or Mac; which mainly processes in series. When IBM's Watson computer became a contestant on the game show *Jeopardy!*, IBM claimed it had massively parallel processing capability, but it was unable to hear and process the other contestants' wrong answers, relate emotionally, or use psychological tactics. Watson's speed of processing information was faster than the humans. The human brain is not hard-wired; it processes with a combination of electrochemical reactions.

The most important point for your consideration is that each of these systems in your brain has high plasticity. What this means to you and me is that the brain can change. When you change the wiring or patterns of your brain, you also change your behavior and habits. By changing your habits, you change your results. Combine this with the newly discovered insights into memory, and you have the ability to become "unconsciously competent." Remember: Memory is emotion-specific, so the more emotion involved in an experience, the more permanently it becomes a part of your memory.

Repetition is the other way that we create lasting memory and develop competence in any endeavor. It is important that you get feedback as you are working at repeating a task or new behavior. If you practice something poorly, that will become the way you permanently do it. The magic is to continually focus on improvement and think about "perfect" practice, not just going through the motions. As you strive to experience new behaviors and then repeat them many times, they will become habits over time.

Attitude + Activities + Skills = Results

"Attitude + Activities + Skills = Results" quickly cuts through the fog of details, minutiae, and excuses. Let's assume you are not getting the results that you want, need, or expect from yourself, your team, or the entire organization. The first logical question is "Why not?" The answer is you have a deficit in one or more of three areas: attitude, activities, or skills.

Attitude

The most important attribute anyone can bring is a positive, upbeat, and can-do attitude. There is nothing more valuable. Each individual is fully responsible for his or her own attitude. As a leader, you can improve the environment, create opportunity, and reward achievement so that self-motivated people will soar. You do not have the responsibility or ability to permanently and significantly change who a person is or what his past experience is. You do have the ability and responsibility to create *new* positive experiences for those who produce and strive to achieve. Whether or not they choose to change their attitude is strictly up to them.

Some people are motivated by fear, whereas others are motivated by incentives. Fear is not a healthy motivator for the long term. Incentives are expensive to the organization. After people get an incentive, the motivation wears off and they need a bigger incentive. You want to look for self-motivated people who match the culture and values of your organization. One important point: It is very difficult for people to focus on what Maslow calls "self-actualization" if they are driven by fear of keeping their job, paying the rent, or some other basic fear.

The bottom line is that you need to hire good people who are self-motivated, people who want to be the best that they can be, and people who have a great big *why* for working with you in your organization. When you hire people, allow them to *sell* themselves to you, and why you need them and they need you. There is a sample Interview Process in Appendix II that I have used for years; it is very effective. Because attitude is difficult to measure, the most accurate way to measure it is by *results*. What people do is more important than what they say!

Activities

What people do, for the purposes of this formula, is called activities. Other than results, this is the easiest part of the formula to measure.

KFIs are the primary things that everyone within any organization needs to measure. It is the essence of their personal performance. A worthwhile objective is to be able to directly tie this activity to the results of the organization. If that connection, activity to result, is difficult to define or is unknown, it may mean the person is unnecessary, possibly incompetent, or a relative. (Forgive me, but I have often seen this in closely held organizations. The biggest problems non-performing family members cause are cynicism from other employees and a negative drain on morale.)

The beauty of measuring activities on a chart or graph is that you see trends and are able to identify areas that need improvement. An obvious example from a salesperson's activity chart would be the track from calls to appointment to sales. How many calls does it take to get an appointment? Then how many appointments does it take to get a sale? Finally, what are the sales?

Another interesting perspective is the correlation between activities and results as it relates to behaviors, time frames, and external developments. If calls are made in person versus by phone or e-mail, what is the closing ratio? How often does a person need to have a contact from our company before he buys? What type of contact is most effective? If interest rates go up, how does that change our results, other things being equal?

It becomes very exciting when you get everyone in the organization to buy into keeping these activity charts. They then start to compete with themselves, feel committed, and have increased satisfaction from their jobs. Can you imagine what this will do to your bottom line? This also will help your employees see where they need to improve. This naturally brings us into the third area: skills.

Skills

Skills are the least important of the three areas. This does not mean that skills are irrelevant. Rather, it means of the three it is least significant to achieving results. Just think about it for a minute. If you have a bright and talented employee with a lousy, negative, and cancerous attitude, what will the impact be to the morale and productivity of others? How about a highly skilled worker who doesn't do the necessary activities like show up to work or call clients back promptly?

A worker with a great attitude can learn a skill faster and better, and can make a more positive and productive contribution, than a highly skilled worker with a permanently damaged attitude. Likewise, if you have a great attitude and persist in doing the correct activities, the skills will be developed.

Fortunately, my mentoring and coaching are focused on assisting successful, productive people learn how they can improve even more. When I do get calls for remedial coaching, it most likely is a situation in which a highly skilled worker has some attitudinal issues. Often this can be corrected by getting an independent third party involved. On occasion, it is a very complex situation that needs the help of professionally trained psychologists.

It's much easier, more fun, and a lot more profitable to hire people who that have a good attitude. The side benefit is that if you get a positive person who can't learn a particular job or doesn't fit the culture of an organization, he or she is usually the first to recognize it and voluntarily either looks for an alternative in the same firm or gladly looks for another opportunity.

Use this formula to work with your team. Share it with them and have them help you develop the charts and graphs to monitor activities. When you meet one-on-one with your team, be sure to review the formula, charts, and graphs. Use them as a tool or reference point to set goals, improve effectiveness, and decide on areas that need training, coaching, and improvement.

Take Time to Reflect

As you contemplate this chapter, take a few minutes alone and answer these questions.

1. How deliberate are you about repeating things that work?

2. Do you repeat behaviors that create results or because they feel good or comfortable?

3. What signs, gimmicks, or tools can you use to help remind yourself what you want to do?

4. How might you benefit from having a coach or mentor?

5. When was the last time you asked clients, coworkers, your boss, or others for feedback?

6. What are you doing to learn more about the brain, emotions, or communication?

7. What do you specifically want to start doing? Stop doing? Continue doing?

Chapter 8

Habits

We are what we repeatedly do. Excellence, then, is not an act, but a habit.

—Aristotle

Habits are formed to fulfill or meet a need. You have good habits and you have bad habits. Both are accomplishing the fundamental task of fulfilling a need. Various studies argue exactly how much of our behavior is simply habit, but they mostly agree it is a significant number (more than 35 percent).

The needs that are fulfilled by habits are either emotional or physical, and sometimes a combination of both. Scientists theorize that habits are also formed to enable the brain to function more easily. Just as water trickles down a hill finding the path of least resistance, your brain seeks to solve problems or complete tasks by finding the easiest and shortest route.

The part of your brain that is used to develop habits is the basal ganglia. It cannot distinguish between good and bad habits. In *Emotional Intelligence* by Daniel Goleman, a story is told of an attorney who had brain surgery to remove a tumor. After the operation, he was still competent in logic, memory, attention, and cognitive ability. The problem was he thought like a computer; he was unable to assign values to various options, and he had lost awareness of his feelings. The end result was he became incapable of holding a job.

Your habits will make or break your career, your health, and your personal life. You have the power to analyze your habits and test them against your values. If a habit is not advancing your agenda, it must be changed. Because it is near impossible to completely erase a habit from the structural contour of your brain, it is necessary to cover it with another, better, or stronger habit that will dominate your behavior. This is absolutely a realistic and possible task.

Buy a New House

Have you ever visited a town or neighborhood where you used to live? Remember how easy it was to find your way around the house when you lived there, maybe as a child? Now try and think about how well you would do if you were put in the same house today with a blindfold on. Sure, you would remember a lot, but there would be a vast amount of details of the house that you have forgotten. You physically moved years ago and have since learned all about a new house. You now have new habits and memories compatible with the place you currently live in. Your current memories and habits are much stronger than those habits and memories from your childhood. In the same way, old habits can be replaced by new and preferred habits.

There is a series of metaphors I would like to suggest that will give you insight into habits and how they change. Changing habits is like moving. Once you decide to sell your house and buy a new one, you must take action. The simple act of putting up a "For Sale" sign starts the ball rolling. *Tell the world you are going to change.*

Build a list of all the things you need to do to sell, pack, and then move. There are things you will give up. Don't forget you need to look and evaluate options to buy a new home. *Plan and act as if it were really going to happen, because it is.*

Start to say goodbye to your old neighbors, and find out as much as you can about the new neighborhood as you establish an actual moving date. *Focus primarily on the joy, benefits, and results you will derive from the change of habits.* Now take the simple step, the trigger, of actually moving out of the old place and into the new home in the new neighborhood. *Take one step at a time, and you will ultimately experience complete change.*

The first action was the "For Sale" sign, and then came several preparatory actions and finally the actual move. However, once the move has been made, then a gradual and complete metamorphosis takes place. You find new friends and neighbors, you adjust to different rooms and facilities in the new house, you start using new roads, gas stations, stores, restaurants and places to worship and entertain yourself. In my case, I was raised in New Jersey and then moved to California during my first year of college. Everything changed, I formed lots of new habits, and I even learned to speak differently. You can change if you want to; it is a proven fact.

If you would rather be heroic, think of changes as "burning your bridges" or "burning the ships so there is no possibility of retreat." This will start a chain reaction of events and emotions that will all help you build the new habit. The decision, trigger, or start of the habit change can often be very simple.

Inadvertent Change

Family members of a client were beginning to notice a change in him. He was getting very negative, telling off-color jokes, and seeing the dark side of nearly every situation. His family finally mentioned to him that he was becoming cynical, negative, and unpleasant to be around. Fortunately, he mentioned it to me, and we started to focus on trying to figure out if it was valid and, if so, why his behavior had changed.

By doing a bit of analysis, it was determined that he had changed jobs, was working out of his home, and was now part of the new virtual workforce. To fill his desire to be around people, he was spending an inordinate amount of time with a group of happy-hour drinkers, especially one person who he had known since college who was caustic in his negativity and chauvinistic toward women. All the negative attributes were rubbing off on my client.

Why would he spend time with this group? It turns out he was a bit lonely and meeting this group of people was convenient, being in their company took his mind off serious matters, and they met close to his house. It was a form of escape and social connection. The newly acquired behaviors were not in line with his espoused values.

The first step to change this situation was getting and listening to feedback from others. Then he had to admit the problem was real and analyze the how and why. What was the reward to the habit? In this case, it was a small benefit with a lot of negative impact.

Now, he didn't sell his house and move in order to change the habit, but he did deliberately change his schedule and find some new friends. When he later ran into his old buddies, they were cool toward him, didn't ask where he had been, and became less friendly.

This often happens when someone changes. If you have a group of friends with whom you have certain routines and habits in common, such as smoking, drinking, or playing cards or golf, and one person decides to quit, then the whole group has to decide who's right and who's wrong. If the person who quits is right, then the group is wrong. That doesn't make the group feel good, so there will be a tendency to ostracize the outlier. Change can be uncomfortable.

Starting Habits

Let's talk about how to create a new habit. It begins with having a good reason to spend the time and effort in trying to learn a new one. This can be called your *why*. Why do you want to develop this habit? The bigger your *why*, the better the odds are that you will win and create the new habit.

The why needs to relate to your goals, which are ideally based on your values. The next step is to design an action that will get you started. Some would call this a trigger event. In sales, we know that the ultimate trigger in making the buying decision is based on some emotional consideration that may or may not be apparent to the buyer. A professional salesperson will recognize it.

You will do best when you put your creative hat on to design triggers to get started. Triggers must be simple, easy, and convenient. Let's say your goal is to be more efficient and effective at work. A simple tool that I share with clients is a small tent card that they put on their desk. It asks a question, "Is this the best use of my time right now?" By putting the tent card in a conspicuous spot on your desk, it is easy to see it while you are doing normal and routine work at your desk. This is a classic trigger event.

Another trigger is a postcard with the mantra mentioned in Chapter 6: "I do it now or write it down." Signs of all different sizes and shapes work. Have you seen the popular sign used by people striving to get into better physical shape? It proves to be helpful and very effective when placed on the door of the refrigerator: "A second on the lips, a lifetime on the hips."

A very helpful way to break resistance and increase momentum for developing a new habit is to use a chart or checklist. Each time you perform a new habit, check it off, or jot down a hash mark on your calendar or chart. This will not only help you to keep track; it will give you an emotional uplift. You will create a sense of accomplishment, success, and satisfaction when you do the new habit and check it off.

Remember: Your brain uses electricity and chemicals to send synapses between neurons. These chemicals are very powerful and can help reshape the patterns in the brain, which is malleable and has plasticity. When you develop a new habit, it changes the patterns in your brain.

Rewards are an intrinsic part of making the new habit catch on and stick. Set up your plan so that there is a worthwhile, and preferably an emotional, benefit to you when you do your new habit. Schedule celebrations or rewards as you meet benchmarks and target dates.

When you take an action and repeat it, you are practicing conscious competence. At the beginning of forming a new habit, you are still in conscious competence mode, and the goal is to get to a level of unconscious competence. This means you have started to impact the way your brain is working, and in time the new habit will become more a part of your mental memory. The brain actually changes its physical structure when you practice a new habit, the way a river can shape a canyon.

Stopping Habits

When you want to change a habit or stop doing something that you currently do habitually, you should start with some analysis. You first have to figure out what need that habit is fulfilling. This need will crave to be fulfilled another way or to be replaced with a more attractive solution and reward. A simple illustration is smoking. Smoking becomes addictive because it causes a chemical reaction in the brain that gives the smoker a good feeling or a boost in energy. The emotional benefit is similar to drinking coffee or eating chocolate. Additionally, a smoker will develop certain behavioral patterns that, in time, actually change the memory pathways. Often smokers light up after a meal, when they get in a car, or when they leave the office. The brain will develop memory pathways to accomplish this. You have undoubtedly seen people reach for a pack of cigarettes and a match or lighter without being consciously aware of what they are doing. You might have done this as well. This is an example of unconscious competence or incompetence, depending on your view of smoking. Addiction to nicotine is the additional pleasure stimulant. If someone wants to successfully quit smoking, he must find better alternatives that fill the various chemical, emotional, and behavioral voids left when he makes the change.

The brain is an amazing tool. Just like Pavlov's dog was trained to salivate in anticipation of food when he rang a bell, the brain will notice and remember repeated and consistent environmental conditions that precede an event or habit. These stimuli are a trigger to start the execution of a habit. For Pavlov's dog, the bell was the trigger connected to getting food. Analyze what triggers are being used by your brain to get you to do the habit you want to stop.

The trigger probably relates to your senses. Smell can trigger hunger. Think about when you go by a bakery that is baking fresh bread. The aroma makes you hungry, right? The same thing probably happens when you smell coffee brewing. Hearing may trigger emotion. Do you enjoy background music? What kind of music do you like? Have you ever wanted to dance because you happen to hear some music? Evaluate the impact of all your physical senses, sight, smell, taste, touch, and hearing.

Sometimes triggers relate to other needs. Maybe you are lonely and looking for someone to talk to, so you spend your time between appointments checking out all your social media accounts. Working as a mentor to CEOs and executives, the habit I find most interesting is that of working late and spending inordinate amounts of time at work or in the office. Experience has shown that often, but not always, working so much comes from the pain endured by the executive when he or she goes home. It could be a reaction to an unsuccessful marriage, a child with severe difficulties, or some other situation. At the office, they are the boss; at home, they are not.

Each and every habit is done to gain a reward or avoid some form of pain. To be successful with creating new ones, you need to provide a personal reward. If you want to stop a particular habit you will do best when you are able to replace or provide a similar or even more exciting reward from some other source.

Keystone Habit

A keystone habit is influential and has the ability to ignite a chain reaction, create other tendencies, and transform all patterns. This concept is discussed in *The Power of Habit* by Charles Duhigg with an example from Alcoa under the leadership of Paul O'Neill. O'Neill dramatically turned the company around from a losing position into a streamlined and profitable entity. The keystone habit he focused on was building accountability and communication about safety, and directly connecting it to profits. Gradually, it caused a sea change within the company.

The best keystone habit that I have seen and that I helped implement in scores of companies is that of regular one-to-one meetings between leaders and their direct reports. Consistency with one-to-one meetings will dramatically change and improve communication, focus, and performance. The positive impact my clients have gotten to their bottom line results is truly remarkable.

This habit should be modeled by the CEO and all of top management, and trickle down through every part of an organization. It will have the best results when it becomes a part of your culture: "It's just the way we do things around here." The magic is to make it a habit, not just something you do occasionally when there are problems to be resolved or new initiatives to be implemented.

There are many styles and approaches to leadership, most of which are a reflection of the leader's values. If you want to maximize the impact of one-to-one meetings on your organization, then think of yourself as a coach. Avoid being perceived as a dictator, servant, or best friend. When everyone within an organization has the intention of trying to help, assisting and coaching each other it is truly a beautiful thing. It reminds me of the Neil Diamond hit "Beautiful Noise!"

How to Be a Coach

It takes a very special person to be a good coach. Most people are primarily concerned with how they are playing the game, working out their job duties, or developing their political position within their organization. They don't have the interest, time, or ability to coach someone else. But you are probably unique, or you wouldn't be reading this book. Let's assume for at least the next few minutes that you are special and very interested in how to be a coach.

Coaching without titles

The first thing you must realize is that you don't need a title to be a coach. When you work at being the best you can be, other people will notice. As they see you setting a good example and achieving your goals, they will have a desire to find out how you do it. They may be reserved or shy at first, but you will notice they are looking to you with positive expectations. The basis of the relationship is their need to achieve their own goals, coupled with respect for you and your ability or knowledge in a specific field. This is more than thinking of you as the boss.

Surprising to some is the reality that you may have an opportunity to coach people above you in your organization as well. If your intention is to help people, this might happen often. Each person has different strengths. When people needs to improve in a specific area, they may seek out someone above or below them. When this openness and candor starts to radiate throughout the organization, everyone wins. People must feel safe with you when and if they expose their weakness or need. This principle applies to people above and below you within your organization, and in your personal life.

Character traits

If you have developed character traits that include empathy and trustworthiness, people will naturally be drawn to you and will ask you to be their coach because they can sense these traits in you. People seem to know intuitively if your intention is to help and encourage them, or if it is to cut them down to size.

Respect for the uniqueness of each individual is another prerequisite to becoming a good coach. Much of this respect for diversity requires awareness and sensitivity. Here are a few specifics for you to examine:

- ▶ Values.
- ▶ Previous conditioning and environment.
- ▶ Motivational factors (fears, incentives, and internal).
- ▶ Behavioral style (Direct, Influencing, Steady, and Cautious).
- ▶ Areas of intelligence (linguistic, logical, spatial, musical, kinesthetic, interpersonal, and intrapersonal).

Coaching has to do with the desire of one individual to help another. The effort has to be primarily one of building up, not putting down. Some people build themselves up by tearing others down. A coach knows how to read people, and is able to focus on developing their strengths rather than fixing weaknesses.

Questions

One of the best ways to coach is to ask focused questions. The art of asking questions is a skill that requires a great deal of self-understanding and confidence. The other person will learn the most when he or she discovers new truths and insights without being directly told what to do. Rather, the coach leads his or her thinking through the process of asking questions.

A good example of one of these questions comes from Terry Paulson, a friend of mine and past president of National Speakers Association. Imagine yourself walking outside during lunch hour with your boss, and it's a long way back to the office when the boss pops this one on you: "So, what's working for you?" Then she listens and waits for your response. Hopefully, you know she actually expects an answer and truly cares about you and how you are progressing.

Questions will enable you to observe and understand the person you are coaching. Learn to study the nuances of behavior. What are their emotions, personal agendas, and goals? Where do they have blind spots?

Feedback

Feedback is the breakfast of champions. It takes a secure person to ask for help and to submit to being coached. When someone pays you the ultimate compliment of asking for you to influence who he is becoming, handle him gently. Strive to catch him doing things well. Give feedback often. Correct in private and praise in public. Make it fun.

As mentioned throughout this book, charts are a great way to monitor progress. When you use a chart that is posted in a conspicuous place, it acts as a motivator. Benchmark the chart with three reference lines. First, chart expected results. Then add a different line to indicate heroic effort and a red line to indicate the absolutely unacceptable level of performance.

During the coaching process, it's a good idea to ask the person being instructed how you are doing and if his or her expectations are being fulfilled. By doing this you will be able to adjust your own behavior and maximize the positive results for both of you. What a concept: coach the coach! It's a good thing. As a leader, you have to be pretty secure in yourself to actually do this. Try it.

Benefits

There are many benefits to be gained when you coach someone. The biggest is that you will become a better person in the process of becoming a good coach. It will encourage you to set the example and be a good role model. It will greatly improve your communication skills. It will enhance your positive attitude. Best of all, it will build your self-esteem. As Emerson said, "It is one of the most beautiful compensations of this life that no man can sincerely try to help another without helping himself."[1]

In Appendix I, you will find a one-page outline of an agenda to be used in coaching. Use it as a starting point for developing your own approach. Every person has a different concept and approach to how she wants to create her own masterpiece. As Albert E.N. Grey said, "The common denominator of success—the secret of success of every man who has ever been successful—lies in the fact that he formed the habit of doing things that failures don't like to do."[2]

Take Time to Reflect

As you contemplate this chapter, take a few minutes alone and answer these questions.

1. What are your good habits?

2. What habits do you choose to continue?

3. What habits would you like to add to your daily or weekly routines?

4. What habits are holding you back from achieving your goals?

5. How long does it take you to acquire a new habit?

6. Can you recognize patterns in the types of rewards you like from your current habits?

7. Have you developed the habit of writing down and measuring your goals and plans?

Chapter 9

Attitudes

Attitude is an inside job. It relates to your internal locus of control. Each individual is fully responsible for his or her own attitude. Management has the responsibility to create an environment where self-motivated people can achieve, feel appreciated, and soar. People need to know that if they work hard and achieve results, they will be rewarded financially, socially, and emotionally. People who choose to have a positive, can-do attitude need to be encouraged.

Many leaders believe that they must motivate their team. It can become an overwhelming burden if you are taking the emotional responsibility for other people's motivation upon yourself. Never take on the care and feeding of other people's problems, or, as some would say, their monkeys. This is the same principle used in one of the most popular *Harvard Business Review* articles of all time, "Management Time: Who's Got the Monkey?" by William Oncken Jr. and Donald L. Wass.

This article was originally printed in 1974 and was then published again in 1999 with an added commentary by Stephen Covey. The original article focused mainly on time-management concerns and techniques for making sure employees don't delegate to the manager things that they should work on themselves. Covey agreed with the article's lessons and added that you must also empower your employees. He shares his belief that it is hard and complicated work. He also suggests that empowerment depends on a trusting relationship between a manager and his or her employee.

Some would say that perception is everything. The way your team perceives they are received and embraced within your organization is the most important litmus test to validate a positive environment. The indicators from your team of this type of culture are high energy, employees who frequently suggest ideas for improvement, and positive financial results.

Focus on Behavior

When people are self-motivated, they will compete primarily against themselves. That means they are continually trying to improve over their last best effort. There is no limitation on how much or how well they perform; they won't coast. Their point of view is that they can always improve. That's why winners love to be measured. Losers prefer to put in required hours, blame other people and circumstances, or claim to be too busy to keep records. It is important to use measurement for all the people in your organization. Ideally, each person will measure him- or herself. This is the bedrock of creating a positive and high-energy work place.

There are at least three very simple, deliberate, and controllable ways you can encourage self-measurement. First and foremost, people will notice what you pay attention to, what you comment on, and what things influence you and are used to make decisions. Develop the habit of asking people what they are measuring, how they are doing, and how you can help them achieve their goals. This means talking about measurement in casual conversation, during discussions about how the business is doing, and in formal one-to-one meetings with your key team members. Second, when you MBWA, ask people if you may see their charts and graphs, comment on them, give positive feedback where you can, and compliment their efforts to measure and achieve in front of others.

Third, be sure you are measuring yourself as well. It is good to let others know you are also measuring yourself, because you are also a part of the group and because doing so helps you to stay focused and achieve more. The absolute best way to influence others is by your own behavior. What's good for the goose is good for the gander.

Several years ago, I was meeting with Bob, the president of a major construction company. His office was in the front corner of the building on the first floor by the parking area. When we were done with our meeting, it was close to 5 p.m. As I walked through the project manager's wing of the office complex, I noticed empty desks; almost everyone had left for the day.

I was surprised to see that, when I got to the foyer to the employee's entrance at the back of the building, it was full of project managers. I recognized several of them, so I poked my head through the door to say hello. Then I asked, "What's going on? Why are you all here?" What do you think they said? Can you figure this one out? They kind of giggled and then one said, "Bob watches when we leave, and we have to walk by his office to get to our cars. It's not 5 p.m. yet."

Remember: It is all about what you pay attention to. Your subtle behaviors, what you notice, what you ask about, or the words you use reveal your values and indicate your intention. Are your behaviors, questions, and words wrapped with positive intentions?

Dealing with Negative Attitudes

Negative attitudes take many forms. An attitude is negative if it is not helping advance or uplift people in the organization. People who are always or often whining about how hard they are working, complaining about the many hours they are putting in at work, or using excuses to explain why something is not done in a timely manner are displaying a negative attitude. Some would call this "loser behavior."

Winners are continually focusing on how to solve problems, how to be creative, and what needs to be done next. Your employees receive a paycheck to solve problems and achieve results, not to complain or simply point out defects. One of the most conspicuous characteristics of a person with a positive attitude is that he or she is always encouraging others, as opposed to someone who is perpetually criticizing and finding fault. A very wise executive once told me, "If an employee is not making your job easier, they should probably be fired." Of all the virtues and talents an employee can bring to the party, attitude is number one!

What happens when people go through the motions of their job with a sour attitude? How about if they are highly educated and technically astute, and have years of experience, but are best known for their cynical or negative attitude? I'm sure you'd agree that of the three—attitude, activities, and skills—the person's positive attitude is the most important. Attitude is a reflection of the internal quality and character of the person, as well as, in large part, a reflection of the emotional state of the person.

Every organization has certain defined ways of doing things. The culture of the organization can often be refined down to a few slogans, mantras, or verbalized principles that reinforce the attitudes and culture of the organization. A few of the adages I heard many times in the military are: "We are not a correctional institution"; "Duty, honor, country"; and "Ours is not to reason why, ours is just to do or die." These types of slogans and sayings need to be repeated over and over. They will influence thinking and behavior. Be sure the actual things being repeated are compatible with the values and the culture of your organization. Common sayings, if repeated enough, can influence and drive your culture either up or down.

The United States Air Force has refined the behavior modification process. As a student pilot, I found every day had a rigid routine. We would arrive in the briefing room before sunrise. The first item on the agenda was always the same: being drilled by the instructors. They would call out an emergency—engine fire light, tire blowout on take-off, or hydraulic warning light—and then a student's name. The young officer whose name was called would quickly stand, snap to a brace, and recite the precisely memorized behavioral response to the emergency. We also practiced locating all the cockpit switches, handles, and circuit breakers with a blindfold on to simulate what to do if the cockpit filled with smoke or you lost all electrical power during a night sortie. This type of conditioning will, in time, affect a person's attitude. It will teach you what to do during a crisis, but it will also improve your confidence, make responses automatic, and develop a safer pilot.

During USAF pilot training, my class lost two student pilots in two separate aircraft accidents. By graduation time, the class of remaining students had been reduced in number by almost half. What is most interesting for you and the purpose of this book is why the majority of the eliminated student pilots were washed out. The most common problem was making poor or unsafe decisions, especially in tight situations like turn-to-final and landing. For a fighter pilot, the killers are lack of good judgment and decisiveness, the inability to process multiple things quickly while remaining calm, and, last but not least, taking unsafe risks. As they say, "There are no old, bold pilots." They had the necessary knowledge and had passed written tests, but they still got washed out. Decisions are a combination of information, knowledge, and emotional factors. Emotional intelligence plays a huge role in decision-making, and this has everything to do with attitude. The ideal blend of confidence, assertiveness, and caution needs to be combined with a heavy dose of common sense. The majority of people fall short.

I have personally known, spoken to, and had candid, reflective con-versations with numerous pilots who have either had aircraft accidents or been shot down in combat. Some were rescued, and several became prisoners of war. It is uncanny how often poor decision-making played a role in their unfortunate circumstances. "Although some think that poor weather conditions or mechanical problems are the number one cause of aircraft accidents, pilot error or cockpit error is the most common cause of aircraft accidents today," reports Lewis and Tompkins, a plaintiff law firm with offices in Washington, D.C.[1]

Historically, people believed that experience and information were the most important elements of good decision-making. You can memo-rize emergency procedures if you are a pilot, or the Latin names for body parts and ailments if you are a physician. However, during the last few decades, scientists have concluded that good decision-making is also dependent on a high level of emotional intelligence. The beginning of emotional intelligence is being aware of self and being able to manage your own emotions. Your attitude is important and a reflection of your emotional intelligence.

As you focus on business development, help your team develop in the three basic areas of attitude, activities, and skills. For some functions, it would be beneficial to do intensive training, especially in handling sales calls, customer service, or interpersonal communication situations. These efforts help with specific skills, and they can dramatically affect attitude. When was the last time you or your team spent significant time practicing skills, and worked on how to accomplish difficult activities or how to control attitudinal reactions?

People believe what they believe in large measure based on their past experience. As we know from science, memory is emotion-specific. There-fore, depending upon the positive or negative emotions of the experi-ences we have in our past, going all the way back to earliest childhood, it is impossible to not have it reflect on our current behavior. When you practice and give feedback to new, focused, and positive behaviors, you are actually building up and strengthening your memory bank. This will gradually improve your attitude. Did you ever notice how good you feel after a good exercise workout? Attitudes are developed the same way we develop muscle; exercises focused on attitude improvement will strengthen your mental and emotional capabilities.

Adapt, Improvise, and Overcome

Disappointment is when reality does not meet expectation. It would be unrealistic to suggest that everyone is always or should always be positive and in a good mood. As the old bumper sticker says, "Stuff happens." We all have downers, mistakes, and mishaps. The key you need to remember is that it isn't what happens to you that matters: it's what you do about it.

Reality would suggest that it is actually a rare occurrence when things work out exactly the way you planned. Sometimes you fall short, sometimes you exceed your expectations, and once in a while you hit a bull's-eye. The world is not black and white. It is several shades of gray and full of various colors.

Recently, I was meeting with a client, a partner with a big four accounting firm; he was concerned about how other partners were unhappy because they weren't getting exactly what they wanted from his department. The reality was that he was struggling with limited resources within the firm, so everyone couldn't have exactly what they wanted. Things were getting a bit ugly, because some of the partners had a tendency to be impatient and pulled rank when they didn't get what they wanted—not that different from a child on the playground throwing a tantrum or running to the teacher when he doesn't get what he wants.

His firm has a matrix organizational structure, so the lines of authority and responsibility are sometimes obfuscated. The other reality was that the partner I was dealing with did not have complete authority and responsibility to make several of the decisions that he was being tasked to complete. Understandably, he was a bit frustrated.

As we worked through the issue, it became obvious that confrontation, complaining, and compliance were not viable options. Rather, it was merely an opportunity to delve deeper into the real needs of each partner's request, develop an understanding of their emotional wants, and then sell them on the option that best met those needs and was in the best interest of the firm. Please realize that the exciting part of this discussion was the shift that was made by my client. Instead of approaching it as a contest or competition, he saw and embraced the merits of striving to improve communication and relationships with his peers. As Martin Luther King, Jr. once said, "People fail to get along because they fear each other; they fear each other because they don't know each other; they don't know each other because they have not communicated with each other."[2]

Do you remember the movie *Heartbreak Ridge* with Clint Eastwood? It portrays a hard-nosed, hard-living Marine gunnery sergeant who clashes with his superiors and his ex-wife, as he takes command of a spoiled recon platoon with a bad attitude. One day while out in the bush on maneuvers, the platoon is surprised by rapid gunfire over their heads. They all scatter and duck for cover. Then out of the bushes walks Clint, the gunnery sergeant, with a machine gun on his hip. He gathers the platoon in a big circle and explains that they now know what an AK-47 sounds like. Their job is to learn how to adapt, improvise, and overcome. That's your job, too.

Health and Attitude

There are some things you control, and there are many more things that you have no control over. This simple reality means it is incumbent upon you to observe and study what is going on around you, and work on those things that you do control. You have the ability to control yourself, not others. You have the ability to educate and train yourself; ultimately you and you alone are responsible for your own development. You have the ability to adapt and improvise in any situation you find yourself. That is why it is very exciting and uplifting to know that you can overcome virtually any adversity. This should give you a positive attitude.

Adversity is a great test of your ability to remain calm and positive. Your attitude is a matter of choice. One of the best ways to get through a possibly frustrating moment or situation is to practice slow and deep breathing; this will help you maintain a positive attitude.

The body requires food, water, and oxygen to survive. The most demanding organ in the body is the brain, which requires more oxygen than any other human organ. If your brain doesn't get enough oxygen from your breathing, you will notice mental sluggishness, negative thoughts, and possibly depression.

If your job requires you to spend a lot of time at your desk, then, when confronted with a perplexing problem, you will probably have a tendency to lean forward, bring your arms together, and bend your head down. This closed and forward-leaning posture will restrict your breathing and cause a reduction of oxygen to your lungs. This posture will unintentionally reduce your ability to generate energy, think clearly, and fully utilize your brain. The end result will be a limited ability to solve problems and maintain a positive attitude. Scientists have identified a strong connection between respiration and mental activity.

Proper breathing is a matter of good health; it helps clear thinking and the ability to be productive. Posture is a tell-tale sign of how well you breathe, as well as how healthy and positive your emotional intelligence is. Slow and deep breathing is easy to do, yet many people are simply not aware that they are not breathing well. Stress has a tendency to cause a person to increase his or her breathing rate and to breathe shallowly rather than deeply.

Chris was my business partner when we had a marketing and technology company. I was originally referred to him as a client more than 20 years ago. During that time, we became great friends, and our families knew each other well. A few years ago his wife, Christine, had a series of illnesses and ultimately passed away. It was a long and arduous period that lasted a few years. During the entire time, she had a strong faith in God and a positive attitude.

During Christine's struggle, their son, Bjorn, met a young woman, Natasha, and, as the relationship developed, they fell in love and planned a wedding. It took every ounce of energy for Christine to make it to the wedding, but she did. The next day she had to go back into the hospital. She was fighting multiple cancers and complications.

When she was able to come home again, she was thinking about the future. I want to share two ideas she came up with. She thought of one idea when she realized that Bjorn and Natasha would probably have children someday, and she wouldn't be there. Christine decided to record several of her favorite stories and dedicate them to the children that may arrive in the future. Grandma would be gone, but her grandchildren would hear her voice and feel her love.

The second idea came later. She loved the beautiful harbor in Oceanside, California. She couldn't get out of the car very easily, but Chris would take her for drives. Along the harbor is a winding walkway with benches to sit and watch the boats, seagulls, and sunsets. Christine decided to donate a bench with her name on it for people to sit and enjoy the view. She even picked out the spot on the walkway where the bench was placed.

During this period, I received a call from Chris. As we talked, I could tell something was on his mind that he wanted to share. Finally, he said that Christine wanted me to share a eulogy and sing at her funeral. I was stumped. I have been a professional speaker for years and occasionally I sing, but the personal emotion involved with this request was daunting.

I resisted at first, but in the end, I agreed to do it. And here's the reason I share this story. Christine had an amazing positive attitude, because she was focused on her *why*. She had a strong faith in God.

The day of the funeral, I arrived at the church a few hours early. I am embarrassed to say that I was worried about my voice cracking or emotionally reacting during my part of the service. I found the janitor and got access to the sanctuary and walked around, sat in a few different pews, and became familiar with the room. Then I sat in the front row and practiced slow and deep breathing as I repeated affirmations and good thoughts. They had a slide show and a small orchestra, and I was up right after Bjorn. The entire service was beautiful. It was a wonderful tribute to the life Christine lived and how she shared of herself with so many. I did my part without a glitch. Breathing is helpful.

Your attitude is directly connected to your physical well-being. That is not the whole picture but a very important part. The way you behave and treat your body will reflect and influence the way you think and feel.

It is advisable for you to research and develop a regimen of exercise to include cardio, anaerobic, stretching, and breathing. The results will be weight control, more vibrant energy and strength, improved mood management, and significant reduction in health risks from diseases like diabetes, strokes, and heart attacks. You will also develop better posture, feel better about yourself, and look better, and with increased oxygen consumption, you will have a brighter and quicker mind.

Competitive Issues

Competition is the American way. It is good, and it makes all of us try harder. But it also means that sometimes we lose to the competition. Babe Ruth and Hank Aaron both hit more than 700 home runs and both had more than 1,300 strikeouts. They kept swinging even after striking out.

There is a natural ebb and flow in life, just like there is in the four seasons and the business cycle. The key is to win more than you lose. Your competition may have better resources and more talent than you. What you control is how much you prepare and how well you prepare. You also control the attitude you bring to the party.

There is an analogy used by sales trainers that says where you assign points, 1–10 for product and 1–10 for sales effort, it takes 10 points to make a sale. If your product or service is an 8 or 9, you only need a 1 or 2 in sales effort to make the sale. If you have a product or service that is similar to that of the competition, the product would rank a 5, and if you add 5 level of sales ability, you will sell half the time, your competition making the sale the other half. If you only add 4 of your sales ability to the 5 of the product, the competition will win the sale.

Some of the things you control that can tip the balance in your favor are your ability and track record of developing significant relationships. Two other things that can tip the balance are superior customer service and a great reputation. Yet another is adding a special benefit, a lifetime guarantee, improving the warranty, or offering referral fees. The best way to improve your sales results is to add large amounts of enthusiasm, excitement, and energy.

The blessing of being outdone by your competition is it provides you an opportunity to "go to school." How did they beat you? What did they do better than you? What will you do to eliminate or minimize their appeal and maximize your own? Learn from the error so that you win the next time. Good competition will make everyone better.

Personal Issues

There is no way to completely separate your personal life from your professional life. When things are going well for you personally, it will positively influence your job performance; by the same token, if you are having problems in your personal life, it will invariably have some negative impact on your professional life. As a leader, you need to admit this, as well as take into consideration the reality that the same principle applies to everyone who works in your organization. This requires empathy.

No one is perfect. You, your team, and I will all make mistakes from time to time. Hopefully you have developed a culture where mistakes are viewed as opportunities to learn and improve. It is important that you clearly know the difference between fatal and nonfatal mistakes within your organization. For example, I have worked with several cruise ship companies. There is a code of the sea that if you make a mistake such as hit a coral reef or collide with another ship, you not only lose your command but sometimes your career. Most businesses are not so judgmental. Our culture has changed over time and now most moral issues are very loose, though there still seems to be outrage when people steal money. What about when people steal time or pencils?

One of my clients owned six thrift shops. The profit margin was beyond anything I have ever seen. He sent part-time employees to the best neighborhoods and collected throw-away items. The items thrown away in high-income neighborhoods were very desirable as sale items in his thrift shops, which were located in low-income neighborhoods. His cost of goods was basically that of picking them up.

His secret to success was that he threw most of what he collected away and only sold the really good items. All of his employees were from very low-income areas. They were paid minimum wage. What I found most interesting was the only thing that could really get him to turn into a tyrant was if he suspected one of his employees was stealing a shirt or other item from the racks or the trash. He ran a tight ship.

How clearly have you defined the guidelines for people when they make a mistake? Is it like most professional sports, where there is a defined penalty depending on the type and severity of an error? It is to your advantage to define as clearly as possible what behaviors are acceptable and what behaviors can get someone kicked off the team. A good friend of mine, Charles Coonradt, wrote *The Game of Work*. His approach to work is to make it more like playing a game. That means you have specific goals and you keep score; there are clear measurements, feedback is frequent and timely, everyone knows what a terminal out of bounds is versus a disciplinary out of bounds, and there is great freedom within the playing field. It makes total sense. That's why people will pay to play sports and expect to be paid to work. The more you can make work fun and rewarding, just like a good game, the better attitude your people will have.

If you agree with the saying I picked up in the military, "We are not a corrective institution," then you want to hire people who have high emotional intelligence and a positive attitude. You may also need to give serious consideration to eliminating those who are negative to the extent that they create conflict, confusion, and low morale. When you measure the performance of your negative employees, I believe you will also find their personal results are poor. That's when you want to remember the adage "Hire slowly and fire quickly."

Take Time to Reflect

As you contemplate this chapter, take a few minutes alone and answer these questions.

1. What are you doing to create an environment conducive to self-motivation?

2. How do you measure self-motivation in your people?

3. Do your people give positive feedback about the quality of your environment?

4. Are your people regularly offering suggestions to solve problems?

5. Do you and your people have unique, upbeat slogans as part of your culture?

6. Would drills be beneficial within your organizational culture? If so, where?

7. Are you creating positive, motivational, and innovative new experiences for your people?

Chapter 10

F EELINGS

People who are unable to motivate themselves must be content with mediocrity, no matter how impressive their other talents.
—Andrew Carnegie, Scottish-American
industrialist and philanthropist (1835–1919)

Have you ever awakened in the morning and felt the soft pillow and the warm covers, and decided to stay in bed a bit longer rather than get up to face the day? Feelings are the manifestation of our emotions in our bodies. They relate to all the senses and how we interpret emotions. Emotions are created by the brain and our memory. As the emotions are transmitted to our physical body, we manifest feelings.

One of life's biggest fears for many people is speaking in public. The fear is created by the brain and our memory of past experiences. I remember when I was about 6 or 7 years old, I was asked to read something in a Sunday School class. I confused *thorough* with *through* and the teacher made a big deal of my mistake. My first reaction was to leave the church and never go back. I was humiliated and now, many decades later, I still remember it.

Another time, my fourth-grade class went to the library, and each student checked out a book. Mrs. Broadbent (yes, I still remember her name) had us come back to the classroom and start reading our books.

After a while, she asked how we were enjoying our books. Then she asked: "David, what page are you on?" I said, "Page nine," and she said, "Is that all?" Again, I was humiliated.

The emotions these two incidents caused for me, based on the primary/secondary emotions model, were fear/nervousness, anger/dislike; and sadness/shame. My body reacted to those emotions with specific reactions: knots in my stomach, sweaty hands, shaky knees, and weakness. According to Michael E. Metz, PhD, feelings are biochemical energies in your body in response to various situations, influenced by your past experiences and current thoughts.

When your alarm goes off early in the morning, you may feel tired and then the emotions kick in. You might feel sadness thinking to yourself, "I am undisciplined; I didn't go to bed on time. I stayed up to watch TV; how dumb!" Well, don't beat yourself up; use it as a learning experience. Eleanor Roosevelt shared a wise perspective: "To handle yourself, use your head; to handle others, use your heart."[1]

So how do we use our head to handle ourselves? The answer is the Cycle of Success. It is a fundamental pillar of *The CEO Code*. Let's review this simple circular diagram on page 159. At the top, the start point, the Cycle of Success has a plus sign (+) on the right side of goals. Start by setting a goal, using your head. Then take action. If you go the other way, to minus sign (–) on the left side of goals, and start with how you feel, you will find yourself in a negative spiral down. It is unlikely you will develop focused achievement and success. The core principle here is that it matters how you start. You want to start with a positive goal and positive, specific action, not feelings.

By using the Cycle of Success, you will achieve more, develop new habits and attitudes, and, best of all, feel better about yourself. When you achieve a goal, you will become more confident. These feelings are all good, and they will make you ready and willing to set new goals. This is a much better alternative than sleeping late in the morning.

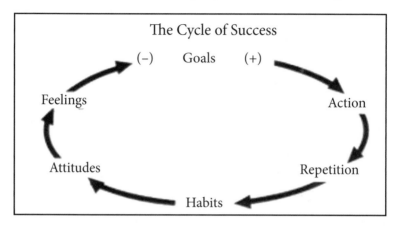

The other big benefit of the Cycle of Success is that it systematically takes you from beginning to end on the levels of competence. This fundamental concept shows how you can progressively go from ignorance (not knowing something) to knowledge and high capability with a task, area of expertise, or skill. Here are the levels of competence you can move through:

▶ **Unconscious Incompetence**—You are simply totally unaware of your condition. (Think of the first time you tried to hit a golf ball.)

▶ **Conscious Incompetence**—Exposure to reality or feedback makes you aware. (You go to the driving range and start swinging, and even manage to hit a few balls.)

▶ **Conscious Competence**—You decide to work at changing, training, and measuring. (You get serious, read a book, watch a video, hire a coach, and practice.)

▶ **Unconscious Competence**—You are now a high achiever. It feels good. (Now you are playing regularly, continuing to improve but have a low handicap.)

During your journey through the levels of competence, you will experience different feelings. Sometimes you will feel good and sometimes bad. At certain points, you will be insecure; at other points, you will be energized. By using the Cycle of Success, you are able to stay the course, aware of checkpoints along the way. Feelings may come and go, but your course is clear. You are primarily using your head, not your feelings.

Read this next part slowly and think about the what, why, and how of your feelings. Feelings are not right or wrong. You feel the way you do, and that is very real for you. Everyone has feelings; we are all vulnerable to them. Feelings are based on past experiences. Each person has a unique and different life experience; therefore your unique personal journey has shaped your feelings. Best of all, feelings can change. If you decide to make the effort, you can deliberately make your feelings and attitudes change. The real secret is *how* feelings change. Feelings change when we create and live through *new past experiences.*

Let me share a quick personal example. At the same church where I was embarrassed while reading in front of a group and mixing up words, I was selected, months later, to sing in a children's choir. That turned into singing in a quartet, which turned into TV appearances. As my voice changed from first tenor to baritone, I was singing solos in high school and the New Jersey All State Chorus. I was able to go to college with a music scholarship and sang all over the western United States to represent the college. After the USAF, I joined Merrill Lynch and built my business by giving investment seminars. Ultimately I created a career as a professional speaker. These were *new* positive past experiences that overwhelmed the mistakes and humiliation of my early childhood. Because of this evolution, I now have *positive feelings* of joy and expectancy when I have an opportunity to speak or sing before an audience large or small. I actually crave it. There is no more fear, anger, or sadness.

At the beginning of my journey, much of what happened to me was dictated by my parents, grandmother, teachers, and others. As an adult, I now know that I have the ability to create my own situation. You do, too. As a leader, you not only create your own lot, but you have great influence on the environment and situation that are shaping your organization and your team. The Cycle of Success is a proven tool for you to use. It gives structure to the process of change and achievement. It is a critical part of *The CEO Code*; use it well. It will make you feel good! As Andrew Carnegie said, "As I grow older, I pay less attention to what men say. I just watch what they do."[2]

Take Time to Reflect

As you contemplate this chapter, take a few minutes alone and answer these questions.

1. What emotional experiences from your youth still influence your behavior?

2. Identify the physiological signals your body sends when you react to intense emotion.

3. Are you ever overwhelmed with emotion? What triggers that state?

4. Where you are on the levels of competence for each of your key job functions?

5. How might you use the Cycle of Success to groom your direct reports?

6. Do you have the power to create *new* past experiences?

7. How will you change the culture of your organization and create new past experiences?

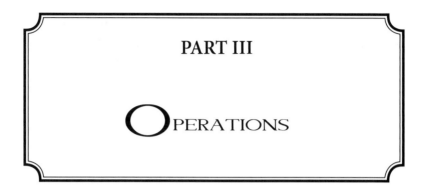

PART III

OPERATIONS

The organized functioning of your business is critical to generate income, build value, and grow. Your well-run business is like a beautiful symphony orchestra. Quality music necessitates having a good score of music to play. Each participant must be in the same place on the score; each player of an instrument must be able and willing to play his or her part. You are the conductor of the orchestra.

The orchestra conductor's role is leading the orchestra. It is not to play the violin as well as the first violinist. The conductor must be astute and be able to guide the musicians, so that they play in tune and at the right volume, creating beautiful music together.

This section will first focus on how people can learn to play together as a team. Then we will focus on the importance of each person knowing their strengths and capitalizing on the strength of others using effective delegation. Systems are the mechanism for each department or group to function smoothly while contributing to the greater good of the entire organization. Clear responsibility and accountability will ensure that the necessary tasks and results are achieved. Finally, the creative application of rewards to the organization's productive contributors must be generous and heartfelt.

You have discovered the secrets of *truer* communication in Part I and how to utilize the Cycle of Success in Part II of *The CEO Code*. In Part III,

I will share proven ways to build teams, delegate, design systems, ensure accountability, and reward your people. Put it all together, and you have a comprehensive guide for how to create a company that inspires your people to greatness.

Chapter 11

TEAMS

Doesn't it feel great to be on a team with people just like you? Everyone thinks the same way. You can relate to them, because they are just like you. But do you get anything remarkable done? It is probable you do not.

A perfect team is not one where every member is the same. Rather, it is one where every team member is different; each person brings unique skills, and yet all know how to effectively communicate. Skills relate to ability, but communication requires willingness as well as ability.

How well have you mastered interpersonal skills? Time and again when I am consulting with management teams, the biggest concern is getting people to work well together. We go to school and learn how to read and do math; however, if we don't learn to effectively communicate, the technical skills are useless.

All people are not the same. Each person has different abilities. A team's critical needs will be met when you recognize this and strive to pull skills from each member based on their unique abilities. Having said this, it is even more important to discuss respect.

People tend to value certain abilities more than they value others. Some of the highest-paid people in our society are athletes and entertainers. Some people believe a person with lots of money is important. They believe if you went to the "right" school or come from the "right" neighborhood you are a better person. Well, all of these ideas have one fundamental flaw. It is the person who deserves respect, not his or her material things. A person's behavior, not his or her possessions or station, is what is deserving of respect.

The cruel truth is it's best for you to work with people who are different from you. You will improve your interpersonal skills, be more creative, and get better results. The most productive thing I did as a young broker with Merrill Lynch was start my own networking group with diverse disciplines in the financial services industry. We had an attorney, an accountant, a life insurance agent, a property agent, a banker, a real estate agent, and me, the stockbroker. It taught me a valuable lesson: An effective team is a cohesive unit composed of diverse individuals who are good in different disciplines. To get the best results, it is advisable to see your team as not only made up of your critical coworkers, but also your customers and vendors. In each of these groups, you must evaluate several factors: diversity, cooperation, attitude, skills, and effectiveness.

Diversity

There is a natural human tendency to like people who are similar to us. An outgoing person enjoys other expressive people. On the other hand, a reserved person is more comfortable with a low-key person. If this tendency is taken to an extreme, it will potentially cause imbalance and weakness for a team.

People behave as part of a group in certain definable ways. When you are trying to start the perfect team you should have diverse types of behavior present to develop balance. As discussed in Chapter 3, the most common model of behavior styles is the four-quadrant model of behaviors: Direct, Influencer, Steady, Cautious. This model is invaluable for understanding and managing a team. As we said earlier, it is easy to learn and very practical to use in the work environment.

When working with the perfect team, each person will have some of these characteristics. Because each person is different, each will tend to bring a different dynamic to the team environment. Everyone has all of these behavioral traits in various amounts, depending on the environment and the group dynamics. Some people will be one way when you are with them alone, and another way in a group or when they are part of a team.

The **Direct** will focus on getting the meeting going, and push for closure and getting results. This is valuable for any group, but needs to be balanced with the needs of the other members.

The **Influencer** will be most concerned with how everyone is interacting. They want it to be an enjoyable process and desire everyone have a good time. This skill is invaluable to present the ideas to management or people outside of the core team in a persuasive and convincing way.

The **Steady** is the mortar that holds the group together. They will consistently perform their tasks in a dependable way. Once clear decisions have been made, they are excellent at follow-up.

The **Cautious** will analyze each decision more completely than any other style. Fortunately, they lean toward perfection, so odds are good that the information will reach a higher standard with their input.

This perfect team will function best when the process runs smoothly. Obviously, each of the styles is different, and has different concerns and agendas relative to the process. Effective communication is the oil that makes the team machine run cool.

The same principle applies to technical skills. A research department may focus on scientific knowledge yet people skills, namely persuasion, may be necessary to acquire funding from the finance department. The best team has a balance of styles, skills, and talents. A good leader will evaluate the strengths of the whole team, and hire or train people to supplement any weakness.

With diversity comes possible misunderstanding. It is important to ferret out and address problems on a timely basis. Keep communication lines open. Regular contact with all team members, coworkers, vendors, and customers will minimize the depth of problems. For the effective executive, frequent, short discussions with coworkers, vendors, and customers are more valuable than a few long meetings or that all-day golf game. People develop trust and understanding by having numerous contacts with another individual.

As you strive to build a diverse team, evaluate your members based on objective results, not subjective opinions. How effective are they with their daily activities and measurable results? Which vendors deliver on time? What is the actual sales volume of each salesperson? Subjective measures like golf scores, friendships, and image may feel like easy and comfortable factors on which to base a decision, but they are not appropriate for most business assessments.

Cooperation

In *License to Lead*, Ross Buchanan discusses research that clearly shows how you could double your employees' contribution. The North American workforce in the research study said they could double their contribution to their employers if there was "more in it for them." And what does "more in it for them" really mean? As managers, we typically interpret this statement to mean more money. But in fact, we couldn't be more wrong. Buchanan mentions the top three things people are looking for from their managers:

▶ **Inclusion**—Inclusion, rather than exclusion, results in a strong sense of commitment.

▶ **Appreciation**—Employees need to feel appreciated rather than being taken for granted.

▶ **Accountability**—Employees expect themselves and their associates to perform to clearly defined expectations.

After developing solid individual relationships, the next concern is developing cooperation. With a diverse team, you need to make a deliberate effort to have cooperation. There are two aspects that we will consider: willingness and ability. Both are necessary, but they are achieved by different means.

Willingness is primarily an attitudinal factor. As a team leader you can influence the willingness of others; however, this is primarily the responsibility of each individual. A person must choose to have a positive or negative attitude. You can encourage another person, but ultimately it's up to him or her to decide to improve. Likewise, you are responsible for your own attitude.

Ability is something that can more easily be taught. Ability is usually related to skills. With training, an individual can improve their ability. This will tend to improve their attitude by increasing their self-confidence.

When I taught Chartered Life Underwriter (CLU) courses to insurance agents, we often discussed technical matters. The highly technical and qualified professionals seemed to struggle to get sales, unless they also had the positive can-do attitude. The sharpest students were not necessarily the big producers; it was the agents with the best attitude who had the best sales results.

A leader must continually differentiate between willingness and ability when evaluating team members. By observation and good listening, you will be able to identify performance problems and determine whether the problems are related to willingness or ability. Ability can easily be improved with training. Willingness is the responsibility of the individual.

Assessing Attitude

Napoleon Hill once said, "No man has a chance to enjoy permanent success until he begins to look in a mirror for the real cause of all his mistakes."[1] Let's look at three specific areas in which it is easy to assess a person's attitude:

- ▶ **Time**—The way one treats time shows how much he or she values it.

- ▶ **People**—Respect or lack of respect for others shows how much a person values them.

- ▶ **Events**—The events a person lists and accomplishes shows his or her priorities.

Assume, for just a minute, that you are a sales professional. Your clients can easily tell how you feel about them by observing how you treat each of the previous three areas: time, people, and events. Ask yourself these simple questions and think what your clients' answers might be. Are you on time for your appointment? Are you well prepared for all their questions and concerns? Have you done enough research? Are you reading them well and are you able to adapt to their style? Are there other events you have in common with your customer/client besides making a sale or asking for a check? How much do you really care?

If you watch what a person pays attention to, you can tell what his or her unconscious intention is. Attitudes are shaped by the values we believe. How do you spend your time? How do you spend your money? These two questions reveal what you truly value. They also show your attitude.

Skills

If you have a great attitude and consistently do effective activities, you will develop the skills needed in your profession. Experience is a great teacher. Skills are important, but even more important is to have a can-do attitude combined with the prerequisite skills. Many times we hire people because of their technical skills and have to terminate them because of their attitude or inability to get along with the team.

Skills can be improved by training. Develop a plan for formal and informal training. Include your team in a process of continual self-improvement. This process will improve both their skills and attitudes. They will be more productive when they realize you are willing to invest time and money in their future.

Effectiveness

The leader of a team has the responsibility of providing its vision. Organizational goals are more important than narrow, departmental goals. Effective leaders encourage people to make their own decisions and take individual initiative. They are able to organize chaotic situations using highly developed relationship skills.

An effective leader has a clear understanding of high-payoff activities and does them. Most salespeople believe the highest-payoff activity they can perform is to be face-to-face with a client. The competent manager will coach this salesperson to understand the value of planning.

A good plan will increase production by maximizing quality time in face-to-face meetings with quality prospects. The leader helps others identify their high-payoff activities and focus on those same activities. The efficient individual does things very well. The effective individual does the right things.

Willingness

Your attitude determines your willingness. No one can control another person's attitude. It is completely a matter of personal choice. You choose to be positive or negative. If you can't control the other person's attitude, how do you motivate him or her to do what has to be done? The answer is deceptively simple: You really cannot motivate another person. The job of the leader or manager is to create an environment where people will motivate themselves. To create such an environment, respect the individual, and believe in them. Great leaders believe in their team more than their team members believe in themselves.

Take Time to Reflect

As you contemplate this chapter, take a few minutes alone and answer these questions.

1. Why is it so important to have diversity on your team?

2. How do you identify the difference between ability and willingness?

3. Do you need to review the four behavior styles so it becomes a part of you?

4. What can you do to improve inclusion, appreciation, and accountability?

5. Are you well-disciplined in the way you handle time, people, and events?

6. Are your teams empowered with a balance of accountability and responsibility?

7. What is your definition of the perfect team?

Chapter 12

Delegation

Time and again, I find leaders who are totally frustrated because their teams are not focused on building the bottom line—profits. I hear things like "They are not doing what they are told to do. Why don't they produce? They just don't get it!" Well, if that has ever been your frustration, how did you handle it?

Did you lose your patience and decide to fix the problem yourself? Or maybe you were concerned about not upsetting anyone, so you tried to ignore it or asked someone else to take care of the issue? Maybe you silently bit your tongue and admitted that if it's going to get done and done correctly, you better do it yourself? I'm sure you didn't lose control or yell and scream, right?

In this chapter, we are going to explore a better alternative. The first thing you need to realize is that you are not alone. For more than 30 years, I have been working with executives to help them improve their effectiveness. Very few of the new clients I work with have an established system in operation that enables delegation to work well. The problem is that often leaders don't realize the *big issues* in production, sales, accounting, and information technology can usually be traced back to fundamental flaws in the way their teams and they themselves delegate.

A simple example may help illustrate my point. Years ago, during a time-management course for one of the big eight (today it's four) accounting firms, a partner raised his hand to ask a question. Basically, he was objecting to the recommended techniques being discussed, because he was customer-focused and had to respond when a client called. Now, we all agree that customers or clients must be promptly taken care of when they have concerns. But I chose to delve deeper by asking the partner a few questions.

Yep, you guessed it. This accountant was very conscientious and arrived in the office early, well before most other businesses were open. He would spend the first hour or so calling his clients, leaving a voice-mail message, and asking them to get back to him. So that is exactly what they did. All day long he was getting callbacks from clients. They were continually interrupting him and making it difficult for him to get things done.

A more recent example comes from when I was chairman and CEO of an Internet company. There is a tendency for some very bright technology people to love programming and really get involved with developing code. Sometimes they get so immersed in the process that they lose sight of the purpose of their efforts, and the need for simplicity and clarity. Add to this scenario the times when they are occasionally high-strung emotionally, and you have a real challenge. But how do you get a bright, high-strung person to see the big picture and be part of the team?

The Solution

I will now discuss a logical and systematic process of delegation that works like a charm. Not only will this process make you and your team more effective, it is also the best time-saver for you in the long term. Additionally, a good system of delegation will give your employees enthusiasm and build teamwork.

When a person is given the responsibility for making a contribution to your organization, he has an opportunity to increase his stature and improve his career potential within the organization. As each individual within the organization is able to handle increasingly more significant responsibility, the power of the whole team will increase. Properly done, delegation will empower your people, dramatically increase productivity, and increase profits.

A word of warning: Serious damage to morale and performance is a natural by-product of poorly executed delegation. There is a significant difference between delegation and dumping menial, unpleasant tasks on others. As with most worthwhile endeavors, delegation is not something to take casually.

The Process

As in most management functions, your first concern is to plan properly. What is the task you are going to delegate? What is the desired outcome or result? Define how much authority will be required to complete the task. Determine who will be the delegatee. Be sure to tell everyone involved about the new role of the delegatee and how other people will relate to him or her.

As you decide to pass a task on to someone else, take a moment to verify that it is worthwhile. One of the best ways to do this is to seek candid feedback from people connected to this area. Do they believe it is necessary and useful? One of our clients, a major accounting firm, was generating a report that was sent to the main office every week. The report took nearly half a day to compile. When we suggested they ask for clarification and if the report is really necessary, the main office said, "You know, we don't use that report anymore. Why do you continue to send it?"

Next, you must design a way to train the person to do the new task. This process should take into consideration her strengths and weaknesses, as well as the personal behavioral style of the individual. Focus on the results you desire more than on the method. Obviously, we all do things differently. The outcome is usually more important than the actual process. When you delegate something you get a *guarantee*: She will not do it exactly the way you would. Hopefully, she will do it better.

Timing is also very important. Be sure you choose the right time to do the delegation and the training. One person will need time to think and process the new responsibility, whereas another may like the challenge of proving how fast he or she is, because everyone handles their tasks differently. Be sensitive to the uniqueness of each person. How do his or her strengths measure up to the needs of the task?

It will do no good to overload one person. The results created from the whole team working together should be the primary goal. Some people are capable of handling more than others, but don't overburden people; it will only set them up for failure. You must figure out ways to help your people win by using their strengths.

The way in which you notify, train, and monitor the person you have chosen will help establish *trust* between the two of you. The art of delegation is really a sharing of responsibility and authority with another. There must be a benefit to be gained by both of you for this sharing to be successful. Warren Bennis and Bert Nanus, in their book *Leaders*, tell us that "trust is the emotional glue that binds followers and leaders together."[1] Without trust between the leader and the team, your efforts to change will produce disaster.

The last step is to develop a simple way to track and receive feedback on performance. Write down the specific results you are looking for and develop a simple system to monitor those results. One of the best ways to follow this is by using a chart, which creates a picture and increases emotional involvement as you track your progress. Get input from the delegatee for the design of your follow-up system.

Authority and Responsibility

Authority and responsibility go together. One of the most frustrating situations in any person's life is when there is confusion between authority and responsibility. This is usually a problem that is easily overlooked, even when it is sometimes blatant.

The manager cannot just tell an employee what to do. It is best when the manager asks the employee what has to be done to reach a desired result. The manager knows and is an expert on what the goals and vision of the company are. The employee is the expert on how a particular job needs to be done. When this sharing takes place, you have the beginning of communication.

When a leader has the courage to sincerely ask an employee, "How is the best way to do this or that?" it creates an opportunity to reward and praise the employee for his creativity. This builds trust and enthusiasm. It also encourages initiative. By contrast, the boss who tells people what to do creates low morale, lack of initiative, and limited results. It may be useful for you to review the section "The Art of Asking Questions" in Chapter 5.

The manager has the authority and responsibility to set the company goals and establish the vision. The employee has the authority and responsibility to provide a specific amount of work, product, or service. Only when the two people have *shared* their experience, expectations, and needs will they be able to establish realistic goals.

The Levels

There are five commonly used levels of delegation. These are progressive levels of responsibility and authority. Gradually, as an individual demonstrates more knowledge, ability, and value to the organization, he or she moves higher on the following scale.

Level 1: Stand by for instruction.

Level 2: Look into it, provide information on possible action, and wait for instruction.

Level 3: Look into it, provide information, recommend specific action, and wait for approval.

Level 4: Look into it, take appropriate action, and provide frequent and immediate feedback.

Level 5: Look into it, take appropriate action, and provide planned, periodic feedback.

Obviously, as an employee becomes more competent, he or she is worth more to the organization. By charting the various tasks that need to be learned in a particular job function and relating those tasks to the levels of delegation, you can assess a person's contribution to the organization. Using a matrix with tasks on one axis and levels of delegation on the other, you can develop a simple but objective evaluation and communication tool.

This simple matrix can then be used during periodic one-to-one coaching meetings between the leader and the employee. As the new employee progressively masters each level of delegation, the date is entered in the appropriate space to reflect their level of competence.

Sample: Matrix for a new receptionist

Tasks	Level 1	Level 2	Level 3	Level 4	Level 5
Open mail					
Phone					
Schedule					
Data entry					
Complaints					

GB STAF

This simple code, GB STAF, is one to remember as you plan any delegation. It stands for the key elements that you must evaluate and then implement to ensure your delegation process works.

G   What is the **goal**, and is it clearly defined?

B   Define and explain the **benefit** to the person you are going to ask to accept the task.

S   Assess the behavioral **style** of the person so you "speak their language."

T   Choose the right **time** emotionally and logistically; "timing is everything."

A   Double-check your own **attitude** and motives, and then those of the delegatee.

F   Design, write down, and implement regular **follow up**.

One of my favorite slogans is "Inspect What You Expect." I recommend this idea becomes a part of your organizational culture. Continually reiterate this simple slogan. It is not intended to be used to find fault or catch defects. Sure, it will help in that effort. However, the preferred purpose of this routine behavior is to discuss progress, uncover any problems, or remove any road blocks that have developed and, finally, to reward successes.

Risks

There are risks in this kind of exchange. Both parties are vulnerable to each other. The reality is that you cannot achieve the desired results unless both individuals are willing to rely on each other. For this reason, it is imperative that you clearly define the guidelines, behaviors, as well as what will be produced.

Workers can sabotage managers, and managers have the means to terminate workers. When the manager and the worker learn to share goals and expectations, they then start to make the necessary adjustments and develop understanding of each other.

The Results

Effective delegation will increase your contribution to the organization. You will be helping others increase their ability as well as developing new skills of your own. All managers need to be constantly seeking people (the right people) who want to be pushed up within the organization. This will develop positive attitudes, emphasize personal growth, encourage creativity, and reward initiative.

It takes practice to learn to let go and delegate well. Be patient with yourself and the delegatee. Be sure you praise the person who has accepted a delegated task and done a good job. If it is necessary to make corrections, do it privately, preferably during your one-on-one meeting.

Rewards

Clearly defined responsibility and authority are not attained by having rigid rules. When respect for the person and the respective areas of expertise is linked with open lines of communication as a result of sharing experiences, expectations, and goals, then and only then will you have the proper balance between authority and responsibility.

Everyone in the organization will be part of the team. People will start to help each other produce and also give gentle warnings when a person is stepping out of line. It will be in the best interest of all to keep clear lines of authority and responsibility. This type of attitude will make your place a great place to work.

Take Time to Reflect

As you contemplate this chapter, take a few minutes alone and answer these questions.

1. Do your employees have clearly defined goals, tasks, and levels of mastery put down in writing?

2. Have you recently evaluated the worth of the things you routinely do?

3. Can people see and measure how they are progressing in their job performance?

4. Do you know and optimize the strengths of each of your key people?

5. Are one-to-one coaching meetings a regular part of your leadership behavior?

6. Do you hesitate to delegate areas that may weaken your power if someone else does it as well or perhaps better than you?

7. How do you celebrate when someone does a great job?

Chapter 13

Systems

Whether you are talking about a simple checklist, a complex customer relationship management (CRM) program, or production and delivery of products and services, the one common ingredient is that they all need a comprehensive system to run efficiently, produce income, and build value. However, there are two caveats. One, in small to mid-sized businesses, there is a tendency to rely on particular individuals to make things happen, and the companies tend to ignore developing comprehensive systems. Two, in large organizations, the tendency is to use the system as an excuse when something falls through the cracks and not hold individuals accountable. All systems need to be established based on clear and specific principles. This will avoid the classic problems that hinder the smooth functioning of the organization. This chapter will outline several of the most important principles that all systems need to meet.

Clear Objectives

Investment of time and money to implement any system is a primary consideration. The best way to make sense of the monetary investment is to evaluate the impact the expense will have on the company's finances, and especially how and when the expense will be recovered and turned into a profit.

Many times, in the heat of trying to compete or adapt to the environment, CEOs make decisions that seem very compelling, but they don't properly consider the timing. Discipline is required when it comes to investing for the company. Timing is everything. Recently, I met with a CEO client who had just signed a new lease. His timing was perfect. At the moment, real estate is in serious distress in Southern California. Because of the strength of my client's financials, he was able to get a very attractive lease: free rent for six months, more than $250,000 in leasehold improvements, and much lower rent than his current location. After five years, the rate is still just more than half the current rate for the same square footage and with a better location. The building is also a significant improvement.

I recall working with a division of TRW when I was CEO of a technology company. The TRW president had a close relationship with another company based in India. TRW needed a complete sourcing and supply system that the CEO wanted to buy from his friend. The VP of purchasing, the VP of logistics, and the staffs of both wanted to use our solution, as it did exactly what they desired and was already built, totally operational, and a lot less expensive than the company from India.

Because the president was directly involved, the VPs were not able to influence the decision. They kept waiting for program completions; asking for the Indian company to make changes, fixes, and adjustments; and just making the program actually work. This went on for almost two years. Finally, Northrop Grumman merged with TRW and the musical chairs in the executive suite changed authority and responsibility. Timing and decision-making are not always easy to master. As I remember the president, his passion was the trips he took and, as he was an avid photography buff, explaining the pictures on his wall.

During the years, I have developed a simple paradigm to help parse goals and objectives. Obviously, goals are a critical part of the planning process. In business, it is important to spend time working on the right kind. Let's look at three kinds of goals for a minute.

Survival Goals

Survival is where you start. There is a relationship between basic business survival and higher goals, just as Maslow's hierarchy of needs starts with safety and goes on to self-actualization on a personal level. Until most of your survival needs are met, it is difficult to reach the next higher level. However, in business, we can sometimes over-borrow our way into believing we are not really in survival mode (just like the U.S. government and some households).

You must be brutally honest with yourself to know at what level you are. There are three types of people in this world: those who know they are winning, those who know they are losing, and those who don't know the score. If you borrow a lot of money, you are probably behaving like the third. The same is true with your normal work routines. If you can't plan your day in written form, you really don't understand your job. Take some time for self-examination.

This principle applies to every area of your personal and business life. How is your health? Do you know your blood pressure, cholesterol, and fitness level? Is the relationship with each member of your family healthy, open, and positive? Do you have cash-flow problems? (Usually this is really a symptom of other, more serious issues.) Are you winning or losing?

Profit Goals

Once you know that you have a high probability of surviving, it is time to set aside profits. The profit accumulation phase must be gone through. You cannot skip it! Yet, how many businesses and people start to do really well and think that "tomorrow will never come"? You must have reserves set aside. One thing is certain and that is *change*. Just because all is well now, does not give you a guarantee for tomorrow.

Growth Goals

Now that you have set aside reserves of time, money, and other resources, it is time to focus on growth. For most people, this is the most exciting time to be setting goals. The secret is that if you have developed good habits and disciplines with the survival and profit goals, your growth goals will go smoothly.

Clearly define your business break-even point, continue to set aside some profits as reserves, and use the excess to fund planned growth. The logistical support of your present business is critical if you intend to expand your business by growing. It takes excess money, time, and energy to grow.

Measurement

Any good system has several ways to establish and monitor measurements. The difficulty is deciding exactly what the key function indicators (KFI) are. If you measure everything, effectively you are measuring nothing. It is like trying to figure out the problem with a soup or stew that has a huge array of flavorings. What is the one critical flavor that makes or breaks the taste?

It takes effort and analysis to boil your measurements down to a critical few. The easiest example to illustrate this is the professional salesperson. The pro spends time on several things: planning, phone calls, Internet, e-mails, meetings, sales appointments, follow-up meetings, networking, and driving—to name just a few. You will find that the most successful spend time on a regular basis just planning—planning their schedule and their approach, and researching the client. This is clearly their highest-payoff time. However, the best KFI is to measure the number, frequency, and quality of sales appointments. All of the preliminary and marketing-oriented tasks boil down to the number of appointments a salesperson gets. This is an activity from our formula, Attitude + Activities + Skills = Results. The next most important KFI for a sales professional is money in the door; this is the result.

When this is measured on a daily basis and evaluated by the sales professional, it can be used to figure out ways to improve results. For example, how many appointments were made per sale? How many phone calls per appointment? How many contacts on Facebook, LinkedIn, and Twitter per actual contact lead to an appointment?

Salespeople that I have coached were able to dramatically improve the quality of their efforts. The real fun kicks in when they realize that their best way to generate more business is referrals. The lesson then becomes that you have to deliver to get people to want to give you referrals. All this needs to be measured.

Let's look at how this applies to information technology, IT. The analytics available today are very comprehensive. You can track page views, time spent per page visit, and even the sequence of pages viewed on Websites. Be sure that you know what your client is able to see based on the type of computers they use. HTML is a beautiful solution, but you need to be sure your target market can and will view it. Many companies block specific functionality for security reasons. Sometimes simple design is best. There is nothing as valuable as getting client feedback when you are designing anything on the Internet. A good source for ideas on design is *Don't Make Me Think* by Steve Krug.

When it comes to using IT to measure financials, work flow, or systems like MRP, be sure you do a return on investment (ROI) analysis before the purchase and have very clear expected outcomes. Many companies sell you a bill of goods, and then you have to spend months and enormous sums of money to implement the system. This is especially true in the information technology field. When I was chairman and CEO of a technology company, I was continually amazed at how insulated and ignorant the "techies" were of fundamental business principles and processes. Spend time making sure you continually ask why they are creating code. They need to know the business purpose and desired outcome before they start. They also need to clearly document everything they create.

The classic example of the yin and yang of this principle is the approach taken by Apple. Apple is focused on design, function, and solutions. Apple has enlisted thousands of independent developers to create applications that give specific and personalized tools for customers. Apple has shifted the financial risk of a particular application development on the back of the independent developer. If it catches on, Apple wins and so does the developer. If a certain application does not become popular, the risk and loss is all on the developer.

Adjustments

All systems need to be continually evaluated. Are they meeting their intended purpose, and what is the cost-to-benefit ratio? Some systems are very simple, as simple as a checklist. In my USAF pilot days, I became a disciple of using checklists. They will not only help you avoid aircraft crashes, they will also help you deliver what's promised to the client and make sure nothing falls through the cracks.

Client needs are continually changing. Staying current on the needs and desires of your customers and clients should be supported by a system of continual feedback. Surveys, opinion polls, and simply asking your constituents for feedback are ideally a permanent part of your culture. Go beyond the idea of only seeking feedback when you discover problems.

Apple created the iPhone not because customers were asking for it, but rather because Steve Jobs and his team created a culture of innovation. They are always trying to push the envelope of new and innovative ideas.

Many manufacturers are realizing that the idea of permanent facilities and ownership of brick and mortar buildings is old-fashioned. Global sourcing has encouraged companies to search for low-cost production. As labor demand ebbs and flows from country to country, those that started manufacturing in India have moved to China. The latest wave is to continue the migration and move to Mongolia.

Several of my clients are having technology and programming done in Mongolia. A controversy arose over Ralph Lauren outsourcing the 2012 U.S. Olympic uniforms to China. My accounting clients are exploring the advantages for companies moving their headquarters out of the United States because of unfavorable tax treatment by the U.S. government.

Jardine Matheson Holdings is a good example of an organization adapting to minimize government's negative influences. They were founded in 1832 in China by two Scottish gentlemen, subsequently moved to Hong Kong, and, before Hong Kong reverted back to Chinese rule, they moved headquarters to Bermuda. Most of their business is still in Asia.

Benefits

There are many benefits to having well-developed systems. A good system will improve consistency, increase reliability, and ensure quality. These attributes will, in turn, increase income, build better value, and facilitate organized growth. It is very difficult to grow without well-designed systems in place.

People will come and go in any organization. By developing systems, you enable people to learn quickly, retain standards, and not lose ground when an employee leaves and a new hire comes on board.

Systems should be built around functions. "This is the system we use to do X." That X can be technology, finance, customer service, sales, marketing, quality control, hiring, or anything else. Remember: Always be willing and open to new ways to improve your systems. The big promise of the various ISO ratings from the International Organization for Standardization is to ensure quality, efficiency, and safety. To grow your business you must create replicable systems for all essential functions.

Take Time to Reflect

As you contemplate this chapter, take a few minutes alone and answer these questions.

1. What areas of your organization need to improve their systems?

2. Do you have a checklist of principles that every system must meet?

3. At which level of goals is your organization: survival, profit, or growth?

4. How precisely do you measure the performance of your systems?

5. Is information technology user-friendly, making an effective contribution to the bottom line, and designed and maintained systematically so you are not captive to an individual?

6. What is your process for staying up-to-date with necessary adjustments?

7. What areas could use a new system? What areas work best without a system? Why?

Chapter 14

Accountability

Accountability becomes real and empowering when you have written standards that directly relate personal performance to the goals of the organization. By achieving these work standards or exceeding them, the individual should understand how it would advance organizational goals. The individual also needs to know that the organization will reciprocate, with compensation or opportunity, to help him or her reach personal goals. When individual performance is linked directly to organizational results, motivation is both intense and self-initiated. As Thomas Huxley put it, "The rung of a ladder was never meant to rest upon, but only to hold a foot long enough to put the other somewhat higher."[1]

If both parties agree on the paradigm just outlined and the individual still does not perform, then it is often simply a lack of ability or competence. Training can help develop abilities and skills. However, if training does not help, it is best to replace the individual. Keeping an individual on board who cannot perform will ruin his or her self-esteem and inhibit the development of coworkers. It will also hinder the progress of the organization. Dr. Jack Weber tells us, "The bottom line is that leadership shows up in the inspired actions of others. We traditionally have assessed leaders themselves. Maybe we should assess leadership by the degree to which the people around leaders are inspired."[2]

On a recent coaching appointment, I had the opportunity to discuss with a client a serious accountability problem he had with one of his team leaders. This scenario is often repeated in the intense environment of an organization composed of highly intelligent people who are focused primarily on one discipline. This is especially common with physicians, engineers, accountants, and attorneys. Let's explore a real-life situation; the following story involves a Fortune 500 company.

Who's at Fault?

Michael, a leader with international responsibility for a major professional services firm, is incredibly smart, perceptive, and a fast learner. Because he is so talented, he is asked to tackle major accounts, and he enjoys the challenge of making deals. He told me that he can't remember ever losing a deal that he made a proposal on. But if he is so competent, why did he ask me to coach him? It turns out that he has perfectionist tendencies, and when working with others, he has low tolerance for their mistakes and errors. Contributing to Michael's angst were two significant external emotional events.

One of his colleagues, a close friend, recently died of cancer. The friend was a workaholic and, based on the amount of time he spent in the office, never really lived for anything but his work. Now, suddenly, he was gone. Losing a friend and colleague abruptly made Michael focus on his own mortality and ask himself why he was working so many hours.

The second event was the result of a decision he made. During the last quarter, he was totally overloaded when a client, the Fortune 500 company, asked him to respond to an RFP (request for proposal). He decided to assign one of his associates to take the lead and complete the proposal. Several weeks passed, and shortly after the submission, he received a personal phone call from the client. The client was very disappointed with the proposal and told Michael so. The client then listed several areas that were done poorly and lacked his firm's customary professional performance. Michael was crushed.

To Michael's credit, he then went straight into the fire. He asked the client for a meeting to discuss the RFP. He made sure his associate, who had created the proposal, was at the meeting. It was a tough, grueling, and emotional meeting. At first, the associate was defensive. Then, gradually, Michael asked some questions, listened well, and finally asked the big question: "What do you want us to do to fix this?"

Michael pulled it out of the fire. They got a second chance and were ultimately successful; they landed the contract. Michael's frustration at the end of our coaching session was what to do about this associate who had clearly dropped the ball on the proposal. Well, what do you think? Whose fault was it? Before we worry about fault, though, let's review what you can do so that this never happens to you, or to Michael, again.

The Solution

Inspect what you expect! Michael was swamped with work, so he didn't take enough time to regularly check the proposal process to see how it was going. When a very competent and intense individual is on a fast track, there is a danger of not paying enough attention to coworkers. Sometimes it is necessary to slow down and check in with your team.

There is a fundamental difference between a fighter pilot and a bomber pilot. The fighter pilot is quick and nimble, and his life depends on his own resourcefulness. The bomber pilot flies a much larger aircraft and is usually part of a formation of other planes. When the leader wants to change direction, he must announce to his entire group, "Starboard five degrees on my count, 5...4...3...2...1...turn." By contrast, a fighter pilot has probably flipped his aircraft around a few times, changed direction, and gotten a lock on an enemy aircraft in the same amount of time it took the bomber lead to make the small turn.

But think of the difference in the result or impact. The fighter might target one enemy aircraft. David Ammerman, a dear friend of mine and former USAF pilot, flew B-52s and was a flight commander for many missions during the conflict in southeast Asia. Typically, he says, each bombing run was composed of three or more B-52s. Each aircraft would drop their bombs and individually contribute to a larger goal. Well-run teams can have a much larger impact than solo operators.

Develop your people! Training and development are continual processes. From situational leadership (a theory developed by Paul Hersey and Ken Blanchard), we know that even very competent workers, when given new assignments and responsibilities, must start from the beginning, and this usually means they need to be "told what to do" until they learn how to perform the new task.

You are probably familiar with the Peter Principle, which argues that people are promoted to their level of incompetence. Just because certain workers are good at one job, it is not automatic that they will do another just as well. They must be trained, conditioned, and evaluated for competence before they are allowed to operate with minimal supervision. It is a process of growth.

Make feedback a habit! At all levels, your organization needs to develop the habit of giving each other feedback. This can be done both with people who report to you and with those to whom you report. It is important that communication is open, honest, and transparent for growth to flourish. When each person is confident and secure enough that he or she can speak the truth, the results are continual improvement. Feedback should be a positive experience for everyone. If someone uses it to demean or simply criticize another, he needs to be coached, trained, reprimanded, or sometimes all three.

Ask questions! The most effective way to sell is to master the art of asking questions. This is also the best way to help people learn. As a leader, your job is to develop your team. This does not mean simply telling them what to do, although it may begin there. Training, however, needs to be mostly helping them think and grow through inquiry. Peter Drucker was a firm believer in asking questions and listening. You can tell the intellect and depth of people by the quality of their questions.

Remember: The person asking questions is always in control of the dialogue: He or she can shift topics, go deeper, or help someone discover new things. Be careful you don't annoy or unnecessarily confront people with your queries. Additionally, after you ask a question, remember to be quiet and truly listen to the response. Silence is often golden.

Questions are an excellent way to lead people: What do you think we should do? What do you think is the best way, from your experience, to handle this issue? How do you think our client would feel if we did that? Would that help us close the deal? What are we forgetting to include in covering all the client's concerns? What has been their experience with other vendors?

A good physician spends the first part of any appointment looking, listening, examining, and measuring all kinds of things to help make an accurate diagnosis. For the business executive or leader, it is critical that he or she do the same thing. Prescription without proper diagnosis is malpractice. As a leader, one of your main responsibilities is to know your team members' strengths, weaknesses, and aspirations.

Get buy-in! The best way to get people to commit, decide, and act is to ask questions. When you do this, it is an opportunity for others to share and reveal their concerns and issues. This is very important when you are striving to express empathy. It is not effective to attack, criticize, or demean people. It is much better to understand their knowledge of the issues and then, through the art of inquiry, determine how best to correct or enable them to achieve, decide, and buy. Any good coach will use this method to help his clients. Remember: As a leader you are a coach. But don't forget that often you learn from others, including those that report to you. Last, and perhaps most importantly, become a great listener. That was one of Michael's secrets and why he was able to save the day and win the proposal.

So, who was at fault? My vote goes for Michael. My confidence is also in Michael; he was smart enough and secure in his own skin to ask the client what they wanted and what should be changed. He then sought help to create changes in his own behavior so this never happens again. Mistakes are an opportunity to learn and grow. Is that the culture in your organization?

Sharing Goals

Sharing goals, using charts, and playing games to foster healthy competition are three practical ideas that can be used to help clarify who is responsible and who is accountable for tasks. Ralph Waldo Emerson once described enthusiasm this way: "Every great and commanding movement is the triumph of enthusiasm. Nothing great was ever achieved without it."[3]

Leaders need to help their team members define their personal goals. They can then help them interpret the relationship between these personal goals and those of the organization. People who see a direct correlation between their personal aims and their contribution to the accomplishments of the organization will be enthusiastic and thus have a large stake in helping the company reach its goals. Implicit in this simple concept of interrelated goals is the relationship between trust and confidence. Trust and confidence are only developed after a period of time spent together. It requires honest sharing and accountability to each other.

Using Charts

Charts are a good way to systematically observe your development toward personal or organizational goals. Pay particular attention to the trends that charts show. This way, you can catch exceptions before they become a crisis. Ideally, every person in an organization will have a performance chart that shows if he or she "wins" or "loses" each day, based on a measure that directly relates to the organization's primary goals.

Playing Games

People will put more effort into playing a game than they will into work. There are certain characteristics about games that people like. We keep score and all the players know how to keep their own score. The rules are clearly defined and feedback is usually immediate. Finally, you always know what has to be done to win.

An emotional dynamic takes place that excites and energizes people during games. Think of the last two minutes of a closely contested hockey game. The energy unleashed is simply electrifying! But can you imagine the atmosphere if the rules and the method of keeping score changed each period? There would be confusion, complaining, frustration, and even more fights. Well-designed games and contests are a great way to build teamwork and tap into dynamic energy from your team.

I suggest that you develop charts, games, and contests for all levels of your organization. Make the type and format consistent with the style of the group. And make them fun. The rewards will be higher productivity, increased profits, and improved teamwork. Desire plus goals equals results. We all want to be successful, and that positive desire should be channeled into specific goals.

Individuals need goals, as do organizations. Management needs to ensure that there is a coming together of the aims of the two groups. A great way to keep score in this game of achieving goals is to use charts that are updated personally by each individual player. Keep the charts simple and make it fun. Accountability is now both obvious and personal.

Feedback

Feedback is a two-way street. It should flow down the organization from management to employee, as well as up the organization from employee to management. It needs to be given in the form of praise and reprimand, as well as formal performance reviews. Frequent, informal feedback is required by all team members. "Inspect what you expect" can be used to praise those doing something right just as well as it can be used to find exceptions.

Employees need to inform management about what works and what doesn't. If this is going to happen, it is necessary for management to listen and answer the concerns of employees by making adjustments where needed, or at least explaining why a situation has to stay the way it is. One of the easiest ways to tell if these communication lines are open is to ask yourself: "When was the last time a worker came up with an idea to improve a system or product?" People will repeat behavior that is rewarded.

Take Time to Reflect

As you contemplate this chapter, take a few minutes alone and answer these questions.

1. What is your definition of accountability?

2. Do people know the connection between their personal goals and those of the organization? Do they clearly see "what's in it for me"?

3. Would charts help you and your team bring focus and energy to productive performance?

4. Given the culture you desire, what games or experiments are appropriate to help improve results?

5. Have you sought out other people's opinion as to the balance of authority and responsibility within your organization?

6. Do you focus on process or results when working with others?

7. When you inspect what you expect, are you looking for an opportunity to give positive feedback?

Chapter 15

Rewards

Rewards and recognitions are a vital key to encouraging loyalty, pride, and dedication in your team. One of the most significant ways to do this is to simply say thank you. When was the last time you thanked someone for doing something? A CEO who shows gratitude by her words and deeds for the contributions made by others will strengthen the bond between herself and her team. This cannot be overemphasized.

Recently, *Chief Executive* magazine selected David C. Novak as Chief Executive of the Year. David, in his own words, is "chief teaching officer" at YUM! Brands. "He believes that recognition is the foundation for motivation—which is the only way to make big things happen."[1]

For him, big things include 37,000 restaurants in 125 countries, dominating the chicken, pizza, and Mexican-style food categories, and handing out chattering-teeth with feet awards to those who have achieved company milestones and who "walk the talk." YUM! was at or exceeded 14 percent return on capital the last three years. Jim Turley, chairman and CEO of Ernst & Young, helped select David for the award and said, "David has been the driving force since the company's inception. It's clear his early focus on emerging markets has paid off. Also, throughout his tenure, he has maintained a wonderful sense of humility during his leadership that adds to his ability to engage his people."[2]

Design a Rewards Program

Rewards and recognition need to be well-thought-out, be designed to be consistent and customized, and contribute to the mission and values of the organization. Your rewards program should be compatible with the culture of your organization. YUM! Brands gives out a small plastic toy (talking teeth with feet) that is inexpensive but proudly displayed on the desk of anyone who is fortunate enough to receive one, especially if it is presented by David Novak. Some organizations give out plaques, pens, or other premiums. The military gives out patches, stripes, scarves, and medals to be worn proudly on the warrior's chest when dressed in his or her formal uniforms. For example, George McGovern, a former Congressman, Senator and presidential nominee, who died in 2012, received a DFC (Distinguished Flying Cross), during World War II. Awards are an important and worthy subject of serious consideration by all CEOs. There are many factors to recognize and reward. Some include:

1. Attendance.

2. Tenure one year, five years, 10 years, and so on.

3. Feedback on customer service.

4. Superior productivity.

5. Safety.

These are all well and good, but let's delve a little deeper into the philosophy of rewards and recognition. People will notice and respond to what you pay attention to on a frequent basis. What is it that you notice, comment on, or show an interest in? Employees are watching you all the time and will try to act in a way that will curry your favor. That is why it is so important for you, as CEO, to be involved in the design, selection, and presentation of any awards and recognition. The easiest way to destroy morale is to have rewards and recognition become ordinary, commonplace, or perfunctory.

The most common example of recognition becoming a negative factor is the "employee of the month." Have you ever been in a small company or department and the people start to joke or draw straws to see who will be the "chosen one" this month? Awards that are not special are worthless and actually cause a negative reaction.

The biggest and yet most neglected reward is compensation. By neglected, I mean the organization has not given sufficient study and rational thinking to designing the compensation program. Compensation must relate to contribution. "One of the biggest mistakes companies make is giving discretionary bonuses," says Mae Lon Ding, president of Personnel Systems Associates, Inc.[3] Because the discretionary bonus is not tied to anything specific, it does little to improve motivation or performance. In fact, it often exacerbates poor morale, because it is not in line with the expectation of the employee, and the recipient becomes disappointed and disgruntled.

Some CEOs use compensation to control employees or as a way to exert their personal power. The preferred approach is to involve employees in designing the program, and thus get their support and commitment. When employees know why they are getting paid and believe they can control the outcome, they are motivated, perform better, and produce or exceed the desired results. People who exhibit winner behavior like to be measured and rewarded for their contribution; losers prefer not to be measured.

There are caveats to be aware of when designing an employee rewards or recognition program. First and foremost, be sure you ask employees for their input in the way rewards will be handled, what the rewards will be given for, and how it will affect their performance and the company's results.

Fit the reward to the accomplishment. If it involves providing excellent customer service, strive to demonstrate good customer service in the presentation and characteristics of the reward. Personalize it as much as possible. For good customer service, give a dinner gift certificate to the finest restaurant in town for the recipient and a guest. When an individual in IT makes a contribution that is significant, give him or her a new technology device or an all-expenses paid trip to a technology show in Las Vegas (assuming it is a very big contribution).

Be aware of how powerful rewards can be. One of my clients, a major concrete structures contractor, gave away a large-screen television to the individual with the best safety record during a given period of time. The unintended consequence was that some accidents were not reported, because everyone wanted to win the big screen TV.

Take into consideration the impact on other employees and customers when you give performance rewards. A major bank had a lot of waste when they started giving awards for the most new accounts. Some tellers began opening multiple accounts for everyone in a family and a separate account for savings, certificates, checking, and IRAs. Be conscious of how you will measure the performance. You don't want to create problems for customers or other employees.

Kevin Hartman, former president of Con-way Freight Western with revenues in excess of $600 million annually and more than 3,500 employees, set a great example of how to effectively reward workers. The long hallways at the corporate office were covered with pictures of drivers who had the best safety records. It was a wall of honor. That was good, but let me tell you the best part. All of his branch managers across the western United States would strive to find someone doing something extraordinary or impactful. They would then write what the employee did and how it got results, describe details about the person, and send it to corporate. Periodically, Kevin would take the best reports home with him during the weekend and study them. Then he would sit down at the dining room table, and write and sign a personal note of appreciation by hand, thanking each employee who made a significant effort or contribution. These notes were then personally addressed to the employee's home and mailed by Kevin with a regular stamp.

Kevin was a client of mine, and I often use this story in seminars across the country. One day in Denver, while I was telling the story, a woman in the middle of the room of 150 people stood up and proclaimed, "My husband got one of those letters!" Everyone cheered and clapped. Then I asked, "What did you do with that letter?" Proudly she told us, "I got it framed, and we have it on the wall in our kitchen."

The Ultimate Reward

There is nothing you can give another person that is more precious than your personal time. It is the essence of what life is. Let me share the following affirmation taken directly from my personal mission statement: "Time is my greatest asset. Sharing time with my family, friends, colleagues, and clients is deliberate and strategic." I would encourage you to use all your developed business acumen and apply it to your personal life. Develop a strategic plan for your family, your children, and yourself.

The ultimate reward you can share with your employees is personal one-on-one time. The same is true for each of your family members. Through the years, I have observed that most executives don't think to schedule serious, committed, and focused time with their teams. My experience has also validated that one of the most valuable and impactful things you can do to create a great company and inspire your people to greatness is invest quality time with them one-to-one.

A periodic one-on-one session with an individual is an opportunity to do several things that are difficult to accomplish any other way. The first is to understand the person, and take his or her emotional and motivational temperature. The second is to demonstrably show how important the person is and how concerned you are with his or her success. The third is to make necessary course adjustments, provide helpful guidance, and reaffirm the goals of the organization. This planned, focused time and considerate personal behavior will be appreciated and will help you become a better leader.

Remember: If you communicate well, it's all about you and the way you treat other people. If you execute well it's because you are disciplined and using the Cycle of Success. Lastly, if operations are running smoothly, it is probably because your people are talented, well-trained, and committed. If you are not getting the results you want, it's time to review *The CEO Code*: Attitude + Activities + Skills = Results.

You will create a great company and inspire people to greatness not because you read this book or know what's in it. You will do best if you read this book more than once and then practice the ideas, principles, and behaviors. In time, you will change and new behaviors will become normal and automatic. You will then realize with great joy that you are creating a masterpiece personally and professionally.

Take Time to Reflect

As you contemplate this chapter, take a few minutes alone and answer these questions.

1. Do you pay attention to important things and people?

2. How much do you value your team? Does it show?

3. Are rewards and recognition part of your well-organized strategic plan?

4. How do your employees know when they are successful for the organization?

5. Are you receiving suggestions from your team about how to honor the winners?

6. Is your company well-known as an exceptionally good place to work?

7. How would it feel to practice acts of kindness to employees, family, friends, and strangers?

Resources

Meeting Checklist

Most meetings have the goal of giving or receiving some type of information. A meeting is used rather than reports or memos because it is essential to have personal interaction with the individuals present to accomplish the goal of the meeting. This is very expensive when you consider the adage "time is money." Here is a checklist to determine if you should have a meeting and then some ideas on how to make it more productive.

	How much will the meeting cost? Multiply the hourly worth of each person by the length of the meeting. Don't forget to include transportation time.
	Can you get or give the information some other way (phone, memo, reports, or charts)?
	Why is the group dynamic so important to reach your goal?
	What is your goal for the meeting?

If you still believe a meeting is necessary, try it this way. Send out a written note that states the purpose or goal of the meeting. Include when it will start, who will attend, and when it will end. Use an agenda that clearly states each topic to be covered with a specific time frame for each. Place the most important items first and request comments from the junior or shy people first. Design questions and seek answers that provide suggestions as well as information and opinions. Usually it is the suggestions that supply the seeds of future success.

Send out a summary after the meeting; state who attended, who was late, and who was absent. Review items discussed and decisions reached. If action was agreed on, record and highlight who will do what by when. List the date, time and place of the next meeting. Remember: The chairperson is the servant of the group. He or she gets pleasure from achieving the goals of the meeting as opposed to hearing himself or herself talk.

Daily Personal Checklist

☐ Plan and review goals (a.m. and p.m.).

☐ Meditate (read the Bible and pray).

☐ Eat five vegetables and fruits (minimize meat and carbohydrates).

☐ Read a good book (one chapter a day).

☐ Do random act of kindness (for family, friends, and colleagues).

☐ Exercise (walk, do stairs, workout).

☐ Take time to reflect (life purpose, enjoy nature, breathe).

Daily Professional Checklist

☐ Plan and review goals (a.m. and p.m.).

☐ Communicate (5 old, 5 new, 5 sales).

☐ Book appointments (average three per day).

☐ Initiate and innovate (push the envelope).

☐ Follow-up projects (inspect what you expect).

☐ Execute (on time, competent, with style).

☐ Return communication (e-mail, text, phone).

Sample Ideal Week

The chart on page 215 is an illustration showing how easy it is to get a handle on what your ideal week might look like. Notice the hash marks, /////, for drive time. (If you live in a busy urban area, this is a factor that needs to be considered.) Next notice the C of I, having lunch with a Center of Influence. This builds on the idea of never eating alone. Next notice the personal items, planning for a date night with your significant other, planning for exercise, fun, golf, and your spiritual well-being. Additionally, there is an item called Sales Mtg. and a few one-to-one coaching meetings with key staff: x, y and z.

How does this sample compare to your reality? Are you spending all of your time in meetings, driving from place to place, or do you have a plan that is productive and also includes your personal life? Leave room for flexibility, and be sure to block time for the most important activities in your professional and personal life. Make a commitment to your "high-payoff" activities and fill in the rest of your time as appropriate.

When you see a "picture" of your day or week it makes it very easy to see where changes need to be made. Paint your own masterpiece.

	Monday	Tuesday	Wednesday	Thursday	Friday	Saturday	Sunday
5	Exercise	Exercise	Exercise	Exercise	Exercise	Exercise	Exercise
6						////	
7	////	////	////	////	////	Golf	////
8	Plan	Plan	Plan	Plan	Plan		
9	Phone	Phone	Phone	Phone	Phone		Church
10	1 to 1 w/x		1 to 1 w/y		1 to 1 w/z		
11	////	////	////	////	////	////	////
12	C of I	C of I	C of I	C of I	C of I		
1	////	////	////	////	////		
2	Sales Mtg				Sales Mtg		
3							
4							
5	Plan	Plan	Plan	Plan	Plan		
6	////	////	////	////	////		
7		Coach Tball			Date night		
8							
9							

Goal Planning Sheet
My goal is:
Self (Why do you want it?)
Specific (Nothing is dynamic until it first becomes specific.)
Measurable (Numbers, time, frequency, etc.)
Attainable (Based on your past performance.)
Realistic (Resources of time, talent, money, etc.)
Tangible (Use charts and graphs.)
Target Date (Dreams don't have a deadline; goals do.)
Affirmations (First-person, positive, present tense, visual, emotional.)

Be sure you state the goal in *positive* terms so you activate imagination over discipline.

My Favorite Affirmations and Thought Stimulators

- ▶ A horse never won a race he didn't enter.

- ▶ Relentlessly abandon all losers—find tomorrow's bread winners.

- ▶ You can't win a race if you stop along the way to talk to the spectators.

- ▶ Early to bed and early to rise makes a man healthy, wealthy, and wise.

- ▶ I am self-disciplined—this is one of my greatest strengths. I make excellent little decisions.

- ▶ I keep myself in good physical and spiritual condition.

- ▶ I am a good listener.

- ▶ I enjoy talking to people about themselves because I care.

- ▶ I visualize myself having an ideal positive mental attitude. Then I practice being that kind of person.

- ▶ I act enthusiastically in my speech, expressions, gestures, movements, and reactions.

- ▶ I permit only positive thoughts to dominate my mind.

- ▶ I associate myself with influences that are positive: people, recordings, books, movies, TV programs.

- ▶ I look for and find the good in people I meet and in every situation I encounter.

- ▶ I seek my goals with passion and enjoy the rewards in moderation.

- ▶ If your knees are shaking, kneel down on them.

Coaching Agenda

Please prepare for our coaching appointment by reviewing and prioritizing the following items.

☐What is going on in my business that I need to talk about? (financials, sales, marketing, customer situation, competition, management team, personnel, culture, accountability, significant opportunity or threat, my role and results, most important priorities for the next 30 days, etc.)

☐What is going on in my personal life that I need to talk about? (quality/time with significant others, friendships, leisure time pursuits, financial, health, spiritual, significant opportunity or threat, my role, results, most important priorities for the next 30 days, etc.)

☐What is the most important thing I need to learn in the next 30 days to be more effective in my work and personal life? Why is it important? What is my plan? What will success look like?

☐Updates on things we've been discussing for the last few months.

☐Updates of key indicators.

☐Review of outcomes for the year.

☐Ideas/applications from recent readings or seminars.

☐Review of My Monthly Commitments.

☐Value of the coaching experience.

☐Other:

Date and time for our next Coaching Appointment:

INTERVIEW QUESTIONNAIRE

Interview Questionnaire
We desire to get to know you and want to assure a proper fit between our new employees and the culture within our organization. Therefore, we ask you to provide us with sincere responses so we may discuss them during your interview. Thank you.

Name	Date

Briefly outline your present or most recent position and business responsibilities.
What would you say are your greatest strengths?
What has been your greatest business success or experience?

How much time out of each 24 hours do you devote to:	
Your occupation	hours
Sleep	hours
Play and relaxation	hours
Self-Improvement	hours
Family	hours
Other:	hours

Interview Questionnaire p. 2	
For you, the desirable way to deal with most other people is:	
Logical and restrained	
Deliberate and patient	
Open and enthusiastic	
Direct and decisive	
(Rate these from 1–4 with 1 being most and 4 the least appealing.)	

Based on your personal desires and financial condition at this time, rate your preferred form of compensation. Circle a number.

1	2	3	4	5	6	7
All salary			**1/2 and 1/2**			**All commission**

What is a good example from your past experience of assertiveness or creativity used in solving a problem?

What are some personal areas you would like to improve?

How would you describe the perfect position for you and what would it be like?

What part of the work process do you enjoy the most? Why?

Summary of Interview Results	
Name	Date

APPEARANCE

Professional attire, neat personal grooming, good posture and body language.

Low   1   2   3   4   5   6   7   High

ELOQUENCE

Executive style vocabulary, grammar, diction, and proper use of the English language. Ability to express ideas clearly.

Low   1   2   3   4   5   6   7   High

LISTENING

Active listening skills, eye contact, patient, able to grasp ideas quickly. Do they interrupt, have nervous habits?

Low   1   2   3   4   5   6   7   High

ETHICS

Is honesty apparent? Do they bend the rules to get what they want? What do they say, value, and pay attention to?

Low   1   2   3   4   5   6   7   High

TEAM PLAYER

Do they share the glory or is the word *I* used a lot?
How do they talk about their old bosses and co-workers?

Low   1   2   3   4   5   6   7   High

CAREER ORIENTATION

How many jobs, and what was time in each? Do they talk in terms of helping find solutions and contributing, or is it "What do I have to do?" What are their long-term goals: promotion, income, freedom, and desire to learn more? What questions do they ask?

Low   1   2   3   4   5   6   7   High

Summary of Interview Results p. 2
MOTIVATION
What do they talk about: challenges, money, friendships, pride in accuracy? Are they persistent, achievement-oriented? Low   1   2   3   4   5   6   7   High
CONCEPT OF WORK
Do they have the big picture or focus on details? How much do they stretch their ideas and stories, frame of reference? Low   1   2   3   4   5   6   7   High
How valuable is their PAST EXPERIENCE and is it on positive terms? Low   1   2   3   4   5   6   7   High

Notes

Introduction

1. Wikipedia.org, accessed December 2012, *http://en.wikiquote. org/wiki/Heraclitus.*
2. Quotationspage.com, accessed December 2012, *www. quotationspage.com/quote/2097.html.*

Chapter 1

1. Quotedb.com, accessed December 2012, *www.quotedb.com/ quotes/4137.*
2. Goldenproverbs.com, accessed December 2012, *www. goldenproverbs.com/au_benjaminfranklin.html.*
3. Dr. Kent M. Keith, "What was on Mother Teresa's Wall?" Paradoxical People (blog), February 20, 2006, *www. paradoxicalpeople.com/paradoxicalpeople/2006/02/what_was_ on_mot.html.*

Chapter 2

1. Quotationsbook.com, accessed December 2012, *http:// quotationsbook.com/quote/15927/.*
2. Quotationspage.com, accessed December 2012, *www. quotationspage.com/quote/28780.html.*
3. Islamqa.info, accessed December 2012, *http://islamqa.info/en/ ref/923/doc.*
4. Quran360.com, accessed December 2012, *http://web.quran360. com/site/compare/tr/59/ch/31/v/18.*
5. Thinkexist.com, accessed December 2012, *http://thinkexist. com/quotes/like/peace_comes_from_within-do_not_seek_it_ without/147331/.*

6. Thinkexist.com, accessed December 2012, *http://thinkexist. com/quotes/like/peace_comes_from_within-do_not_seek_it_ without/147331/.*
7. Bible.cc, accessed December 2012, *http://bible.cc/ matthew/22-39.htm.*
8. Resurrectionchapel.tv, accessed December 2012, *www. resurrectionchapel.tv/love-each-other-as-brothers-and-sisters-and-honor-others-more-than-you-do-yourself-romans-1210/.*
9. Goodreads.com, accessed December 2012, *www.goodreads.com/ quotes/20699-remember-that-the-best-relationship-is-one-in-which-your.*
10. Goodreads.com, accessed December 2012, *www.goodreads.com/ quotes/13401-when-you-are-content-to-be-simply-yourself-and-don-t.*
11. Quotationsbook.com, accessed December 2012, *http:// quotationsbook.com/quote/21259/.*
12. "Politics by Aristotle," translated by Benjamin Jowet, *http:// classics.mit.edu/Aristotle/politics.5.five.html.*
13. Archives.gov, accessed December 2012, *www.archives.gov/ exhibits/charters/declaration_transcript.html.*
14. Reallifechristianityonline.com, accessed December 2012, *www. reallifechristianityonline.com/blog/2011/04/29/65-Let-Him-Who-is-Without-Sin-Throw-the-First-Stone.aspx.*
15. Brainyquote.com, accessed December 2012, *www.brainyquote. com/quotes/authors/m/margaret_thatcher.html.*

Chapter 3
1. Joseph LeDoux, *Synaptic Self* (New York: Penguin Books, 2002), p. 117.
2. Wikipedia.org, accessed December 2012, *http://en.wikiquote. org/wiki/Heraclitus.*

Chapter 4
1. Ocbenji.com, accessed December 2012, *www.ocbenji.com/ blog/2008/08/04/quotes-10/.*
2. Brainyquote.com, accessed December 2012, *www.brainyquote. com/quotes/quotes/t/theodorero140484.html.*

3. Corporate.ford.com, accessed December 2012, *http://corporate. ford.com/our-company/community/ford-fund/presidents-message-401p?releaseId=1244754314736.*

Chapter 5

1. Goodreads.com, accessed December 2012, *www.goodreads.com/ quotes/10800-people-fail-to-get-along-because-they-fear-each-other.*

Part II

1. Erich Fromm, *To Have or to Be?* (New York: Harper & Row, 1976).
2. Brainyquote.com, accessed December 2012, *www.brainyquote. com/quotes/quotes/a/aristotle145967.html.*
3. Thinkexist.com, accessed December 2012, *http://thinkexist. com/quotation/doing_the_right_thing_is_more_important_ than/198135.html.*

Chapter 6

1. Thinkexist.com, accessed December 2012, *http://thinkexist. com/quotation/everything_must_degenerate_into_work_if_ anything/298367.html.*
2. Answers.google.com, accessed December 2012, *http://answers. google.com/answers/threadview/id/742598.html.*

Chapter 7

1. CBSnews.com, accessed December 2012, *www.cbsnews. com/8301-3445_162-57551532/john-goodman-let-the-demons-chase-me-now/.*
2. Quotationsbook.com, accessed December 2012, *http:// quotationsbook.com/quote/5896/.*

Chapter 8

1. Thinkexist.com, accessed December 2012, *http://thinkexist.com/ quotation/it_is_one_of_the_most_beautiful_compensations_ of/181419.html.*
2. Thebirchgroup.com, accessed December 2012, *www. thebirchgroup.com/Portals/129853/docs/Revisiting%20the%20 Common%20Denominator%20of%20Success.pdf.*

Chapter 9

1. Lewisandtompkins.com, accessed December 2012, *www. lewisandtompkins.com.*

2. Goodreads.com, accessed December 2012, *www.goodreads.com/ quotes/10800-people-fail-to-get-along-because-they-fear-each- other.*

Chapter 10

1. Goodreads.com, accessed December 2012, *www.goodreads. com/quotes/142537-to-handle-yourself-use-your-head-to-handle- others-use.*

2. Thinkexist.com, accessed December 2012, *http://thinkexist. com/quotation/as_i_grow_older-i_pay_less_attention_to_what_ men/151029.html.*

Chapter 11

1. Knowtheflow.ca, accessed December 2012, *www.knowtheflow. ca/tag/napoleon-hill/.*

Chapter 12

1. Warren Bennis and Bert Nanus, *Leaders: Strategies for Taking Charge* (New York: HarperCollins, 2003).

Chapter 14

1. Brainyquotes.com, accessed December 2012, *www.brainyquote. com/quotes/quotes/t/thomashux1101466.html.*

2. Getsynthesis.com, accessed December 2012, *http:// getsynthesis.com/fusion/index.php?option=com_ content&task=view&id=71&Itemid=92.*

3. Discospock.com, accessed December 2012, *www.discospock. com/Famous_Quotes.txt.*

Chapter 15

1. J. P. Donlon, "2012 CEO of the Year: The Recognition Leader," *Chief Executive* July/August 2012, p. 24.

2. Ibid., 28.

3. From an October 2012 phone conversation with the author.

BIBLIOGRAPHY

Bennis, Warren, and Bert Nanus. *Leaders: Strategies for Taking Charge.* New York: HarperCollins, 2003.

Caesar, Vance, and Carol Ann. *The High Achiever's Guide to Happiness.* Thousand Oaks, Calif.: Corwin Press, 2006.

Coonradt, Charles A., and Lee Nelson. *The Game of Work.* Orem, Utah: Liberty Press, 1984.

Donlon, J. P. "2012 CEO of the Year: The Recognition Leader," *Chief Executive.* Greenwich, Conn.: Chief Executive Group, LLC. July/August 2012. No. 259.

Fromm, Erich. *To Have or to Be?* New York: Harper & Row, 1976.

Goleman, Daniel. *Emotional Intelligence.* New York: Bantam Books, 1997.

LeDoux, Joseph. *Synaptic Self: How Our Brains Become Who We Are.* New York: Penguin Books, 2002.

McGaugh, James. *Memory and Emotion: The Making of Lasting Memories.* New York: Columbia University Press, 2003.

Tickle, Naomi. *It's All in the Face: The Facts and Fantasies of Face Reading.* Wichita, Kan.: Daniels Publishing, 1995.

INDEX

ABOUT THE AUTHOR

D AVID ROHLANDER is a mentor, a coach, and a professional speaker. David has coached partners for Ernst & Young, trained sales teams with Honeywell, and mentored hundreds of CEOs and executives in a wide range of industries both nationally and internationally. As a professional speaker he has presented in North, South, and Central America, Europe, and on cruise ships to thousands of people for Fortune 100 companies, associations, governments, and small to mid-sized businesses. His delivery style is friendly and warm while simultaneously being tough in-your-face, which is the perfect combination to gain credibility while instituting drastic change or paradigm shifts.

Rohlander's unique blend of expertise and experience includes being the founder and CEO of three companies, appointment to Merrill Lynch's Management Advisory Council, and 208 combat missions as a U.S. Air Force fighter pilot. David earned an MBA in finance from California State University and studied management with Peter Drucker at Claremont Graduate University. He lives in Orange County, California.

To reach David for information about his speaking, training, or coaching, visit his Website at *www.DavidRohlander.com*, e-mail him at David@DavidRohlander.com, or call his office at (714) 771-7043.